The Low Gi Diet Cookbook

The Low Gi Diet Cookbook

100 delicious low GI recipes to help you lose weight and keep it off

Dr Jennie Brand-Miller, the authority on low GI eating

Kaye Foster-Powell and Joanna McMillan-Price

HODDER
MOBIUS

CONTENTS

THANK YOU

When our publisher asked us to create a cookbook to accompany our recent book, *The Low GI Diet*, we decided that we wanted to share with our readers the low GI foods and recipes we love to cook ourselves, at home. All the recipes in this book come from the real world—our own kitchens, and those of our families, friends and colleagues. We also asked some leading chefs and food writers for recipes—so a special thank you to Antonio Carluccio, Judy Davie, Margaret Fulton, Julie Le Clerc, Luke Mangan, Catherine Saxelby, Carol Selva Rajah, Rosemary Stanton, Rick Stein, Michelle Trute and Loukie Werle for generously agreeing to let us reproduce their recipes in our book.

High in nutrition and full of flavour, the low GI recipes we have chosen are rich in lean proteins, good fats, vital vegetables and healthy wholegrains. It should not surprise you that the recipes represent a way of eating that's part and parcel of many ethnic cuisines. Having stood the test of time, they are naturally and simply delicious.

We are very fortunate in our families and friends. Thank you to everyone who shared their favourite recipes and for their help in creating this book with us. It's been fun. We have to say a special thank you to Joanna's mum, Isobel McMillan, who travelled from Scotland to Sydney for a month to help with a new baby and was set to work creating and testing low GI recipes in her 'time off'.

A very special thank you also to Jenny Fanshaw for her hard work testing all the recipes. We really appreciated her help in meeting our deadlines.

And finally, our thanks, as always, to Philippa Sandall, our wonderful agent and so much more! She sourced and contributed many of the recipes, and we are indebted to her for all her advice and expertise in helping to create such a fabulous book.

Jennie, Kaye & Joanna

Author photograph: (from left to right) Kaye Foster-Powell,
Joanna McMillan-Price, Prof Jennie Brand-Miller

INTRODUCTION

In *The Low GI Diet Cookbook*, a practical companion to our 12-week weight-loss action plan, *The Low GI Diet,* you will find 100-plus recipes for breakfast, lunch, dinner, those snacks in between, and some delicious desserts to help you put the GI to work in your kitchen—and throughout your day.

For those of you who have read *The Low GI Diet*, you will already know that you can eat plenty of fruit and vegetables (go easy on potatoes), plus sensible quantities of bread, pasta, noodles, breakfast cereal, rice and wholegrains—the low GI ones of course. On The Low GI Diet™ you can also enjoy lean meat, poultry, fish, shellfish, eggs and low fat dairy foods such as milk, cheese and yoghurt. And you will also know that legumes play a starring role because they have the lowest GI of all.

For those of you who have just picked up this book, you will discover that The Low GI Diet™ is not low fat or low carb or high protein. It's the safe, delicious and satiating weight-loss plan that gets an approving nod from nutritionists the world over. We like to describe it as a carbohydrate-controlled diet because it is based on choosing low GI carbs that are slowly digested and absorbed, producing only gentle rises in your blood glucose and insulin levels. Lowering your insulin levels is not only a key ingredient in weight loss, but also the secret to long-term health.

WHY THE LOW GI DIET WORKS

Low GI foods have the unique ability to keep you feeling fuller for longer and to maximise your engine revs (metabolic rate) during active weight loss. And, as we all know, the higher your metabolic rate, the easier your weight loss. By slowing down digestion and absorption of carbohydrates, The Low GI Diet™ steadies both your blood glucose and insulin levels, stopping the roller-coaster ride that spells hunger and bingeing. And by bringing down insulin, your body will burn more body fat.

THE SEVEN GUIDELINES OF THE LOW GI DIET

We believe that choosing low GI foods is one of the most important dietary choices you can make for your long-term health, energy and weight control. As well as identifying your best low GI choices, our guidelines give you a blueprint for healthy eating for life.

1 EAT SEVEN OR MORE SERVINGS OF FRUIT AND VEGETABLES EVERY DAY

Being high in fibre, and therefore filling, and low in fat (apart from olives and avocado, which contain 'good' fats), fruit and vegetables play a central role in The Low GI Diet™. They are also bursting with vitamins, minerals, anti-oxidants and phytochemicals, which will give you the glow of good health. Aim to eat at least two serves of fruit and five serves of vegetables daily, preferably of three or more different colours. A serve is about one medium-sized piece of fruit, or half a cup of cooked vegetables or one cup of raw.

Most vegetables have very little carbohydrate so do not have a GI. Potato, however, has a high GI, so if you are a big potato eater, try to replace some with low GI alternatives such as sweet corn, sweet potato, taro and yam. As for green and salad vegetables, you can eat them freely, so pile your plate high and remember that variety is the key.

Most fruit have a low GI, the lowest being apples and citrus (such as oranges and grapefruit) and stone fruits (such as peaches and nectarines). However, there's no need to limit high GI fruit such as watermelon or rockmelon because even a large serve of these healthy fruit contains very little carbohydrate.

2 EAT LOW GI BREADS AND CEREALS

The type of bread and cereals you eat affects the GI of your diet the most. Mixed grain breads, sourdough, traditional rolled oats, bulgur wheat, pearl barley, pasta, noodles and certain types of rice are just a few examples of low GI cereal foods. One of the easiest and most important changes you can make to lower the overall GI of your diet is to choose a low GI bread. Most people need at least four serves of grains a day (very active people need more), where a serve is two slices of bread or half a cup of rice or pasta.

3 EAT MORE LEGUMES INCLUDING BEANS, CHICKPEAS AND LENTILS

Whether you buy dried beans, chickpeas or lentils and cook them yourself at home or opt for convenient, time-saving canned varieties, you are choosing one of nature's lowest GI foods. These nutritional 'power packs' are high in fibre, low in kilojoules (calories) and provide a valuable source of protein, carbohydrate, B vitamins, folate, iron, zinc and magnesium. Enjoy them at least twice a week for meals or snacks.

4 EAT NUTS MORE REGULARLY

Although nuts are high in fat (averaging around 50 per cent), it is largely unsaturated fat, so they make a healthy substitute for snacks such as biscuits, cakes, pastries, potato chips and chocolate. They also contain relatively little carbohydrate, so most do not have a GI. The exceptions are cashews and peanuts, which are low GI. Nuts contain a variety of anti-oxidants and are also one of the richest sources of vitamin E—in fact, a small handful of mixed nuts provides more than 20 per cent of your recommended daily intake.

5 EAT MORE FISH AND SEAFOOD

Fish and seafood do not have a GI because they are a source of protein, not carbohydrate. Increased fish consumption is linked to a reduced risk of coronary heart disease, improvements in mood, lower rates of depression, better blood fat levels and enhanced immunity. The likely protective components are the omega-3 fatty acids. Our bodies only make small amounts of these fatty acids and so we rely on our diet, especially fish and seafood, to obtain them. One to three meals of fish each week is a good habit to get into to start reaping all the health benefits.

The richest sources of omega-3 fats are oily fish such as Atlantic and smoked salmon, and swordfish. However, canned sardines, mackerel and salmon and, to a lesser extent, tuna are also good sources. Look for canned fish packed in water, olive oil, canola oil, tomato sauce or brine, and drain well.

Due to the risk of high levels of mercury in certain species of fish, Food Standards Australia and New Zealand (FSANZ) advises that we limit our consumption of shark (flake) and billfish (swordfish, broadbill or marlin) to one serve (150 g/5¼ oz) per week and to eat no other fish that week. And they advise pregnant women and young children to limit their intake to half this amount.

6 EAT LEAN RED MEATS, POULTRY AND EGGS

These protein foods do not have a GI because they are not sources of carbohydrate. Red meat, however, is the best source of iron you can get. Good iron status can increase your energy levels and improve your exercise tolerance. We suggest eating lean red meat two or three times a week (serving sizes of about 100 g/3½ oz is okay in a healthy diet) and accompanying it with a salad or vegetables. A couple of eggs or 120 g (4¼ oz) of skinless chicken provide options for variety once or twice a week.

7 EAT LOW FAT DAIRY PRODUCTS

Milk, cheese, ice-cream, yoghurt, buttermilk and custard are the richest sources of calcium in our diet. By replacing full fat dairy foods with reduced fat, low fat or fat-free versions, you will reduce your saturated fat intake and actually boost your calcium intake.

ACTIVITY—THE OTHER SIDE OF THE ENERGY EQUATION

The Low GI Diet™ deals not only with what goes in your mouth (energy intake), but with physical activity (energy output). This is the critical side of the energy equation. If you don't build physical activity into your life, you have very little chance of changing your body shape for life.

Exercising while you lose weight will help you maximise fat loss and minimise lean muscle loss. This means you get leaner faster. Throughout *The Low GI Diet Cookbook*, we have included activity tips to help you stay on track because we know that the people most likely to keep the weight off are those who raise their activity levels and make exercise a natural part of life.

WHAT IS THE GI?

The GI (glycemic index), a proven measure of how fast carbohydrates hit the bloodstream, helps you choose the right amount and type of carbohydrates for your health and wellbeing. Foods with a high GI value contain carbohydrates that will cause a dramatic rise in your blood glucose levels, while foods with a low GI value contain carbohydrates that will have a lesser impact.

LOW GI < 55
MEDIUM (OR MODERATE) GI 56–69
HIGH GI > 70

HOW OUR LOW GI RECIPES GIVE YOU A HEALTHY BALANCE

We have chosen recipes that will give you a healthy balance of all the nutrients your body needs. We have analysed the recipes and the nutrient profile* includes the GI (glycemic index), energy, fat, protein, carbohydrate, fibre and sodium content per serve. Here we explain the role each nutrient plays in The Low GI Diet™.

GI An emphasis on low GI carbs such as pasta, legumes, sweet potato, wholegrains, fruit and dairy products ensures most of our recipes have a low GI. The value we give is our best estimate of the range in which the GI of each recipe falls.

ENERGY DENSITY The kilojoule (calorie) count per serve of each recipe indicates its energy density. This is important for weight control because it's easy to overconsume kilojoules when your diet is based on energy-dense foods. By incorporating lots of vegetables, salads, fruit and high fibre foods into recipes, they retain a lower energy density.

FATS Forget what you've been told about low fat and learn the new fat message—it's not all bad. The type of fat is more important for your health than the total amount. Most of us need to eat more of certain types of fat for optimal health. These fats include the omega-3 fats found in fish and seafood, and omega-neutral monounsaturated fats found in olive and canola oils. You'll find we have incorporated the 'good' fats in our recipes by using nuts, oily fish, avocado, olives and olive oil.

PROTEIN Sufficient protein in the diet is important for weight control because, compared to carbohydrate and fat, protein makes us feel more satisfied immediately after eating and reduces hunger between meals. Protein also increases our metabolic rate for 1–3 hours after eating. This means we burn more energy by the minute compared with the increase that occurs after eating carbohydrates or fats. Even though this is a relatively small difference, it may be important in long-term weight control. Our recipes include the highest quality, lowest fat protein sources of lean meat, fish, shellfish, tofu and legumes.

CARBOHYDRATE Most of our recipes have a carbohydrate base but the emphasis is always on low GI because the slow digestion and absorption of these foods will fill you up, trickle fuel into your engine at a more useable rate, and keep you satisfied for longer. The actual amount of carbohydrate consumed at each meal may be relevant to those with diabetes and those who monitor their blood glucose levels.

We've used moderate amounts of refined sugar (medium GI) in our recipes for healthy desserts and sweet treats. The World Health Organization says 'a moderate intake of sugar-rich foods can provide for a palatable and nutritious diet'. So, enjoy refined sugar, using it judiciously to make nutritious foods more palatable. Just be mindful of sugar in liquid form (such as soft drinks and fruit juices) because they are easy to overconsume.

FIBRE Experts recommend a daily fibre intake of 30 g (1 oz) but most people fall short of that, averaging 20–25 g (³⁄₄–1 oz). The Low GI Diet™ will get you a lot closer to the target because most of our recipes are brimming with fibre. This means they will not only keep you regular but will also help lower your blood glucose, your cholesterol levels and reduce your risk of many chronic diseases.

SODIUM Sodium is the part of salt that can increase blood pressure. We want you to minimise consumption of salt and salty foods, so, you will find that, in most cases, salt hasn't been included as an ingredient in our recipes. One exception, however, is the recipes by our celebrity chefs. For these, we have remained authentic to the original version by leaving in the salt if it was used. Because many people follow low sodium diets, we have included the sodium content of each recipe. (You can consider a low sodium dish as containing less than 400 mg per serving.)

* Recipes have been analysed using nutrient analysis software, FoodWorks® (Xyris Software), based on Australian New Zealand food composition data.

HOW TO USE THIS BOOK

Two reasons The Low GI Diet™ is so easy to live with long-term are that there are no special foods to buy and you can enjoy three balanced meals a day, including a dessert or indulgence at dinner and snacks in between, if you wish. So, to keep making it easy for you, that's how we have organised the chapters in our cookbook—Breakfast, Lunches and Light Meals, Soups and Salads, Dinner, and Desserts and Sweet Treats. We have also included a section called Basic Recipes, where you will find the spice blends we use in a number of recipes, along with some popular side dishes and accompaniments such as tabbouli and saffron pilaf.

To keep making low GI eating easy every day and every meal, turn to the section called Your Low GI Diet Foods. Here's where we explain what to stock in your pantry, refrigerator and freezer.

The recipes are generally quick (see the preparation and cooking times) and easy to make, and full of healthy ingredients. If a recipe is rich in particular micronutrients, we have identified them for you in the recipe introduction. We have also included cook's tips, with information on recipe short cuts, preparation hints and shopping tips. And, of course, there are the activity ideas to help you stay motivated and make exercise and physical activity a natural part of your life.

We hope that you enjoy preparing and eating these meals as much as we do.

BREAKFAST

MAKE BREAKFAST A PRIORITY—IT'S THE MOST
IMPORTANT MEAL OF YOUR DAY, RECHARGING
YOUR BRAIN AND SPEEDING UP YOUR
METABOLISM AFTER AN OVERNIGHT 'FAST'.
THESE DELICIOUS BREAKFASTS AND BRUNCHES,
FILLED WITH FRESH INGREDIENTS AND
PREPARED WITH MINIMUM FUSS, WILL
NOURISH YOUR BODY AND SUSTAIN YOU
THROUGH THE MORNING.

SCRAMBLED EGGS WITH SMOKED SALMON SERVES 2

This recipe is not only a sustaining breakfast but makes a quick and easy light brunch or lunch. You could also serve it with a crispy green salad as an evening meal. Preparation time: 10 minutes Cooking time: 8 minutes

4 eggs, at room temperature
80 ml (2½ fl oz/⅓ cup) low fat milk
freshly ground black pepper
1 tablespoon thinly sliced chives
1 tablespoon finely chopped dill
100 g (3½ oz) smoked salmon, chopped
30 g (1 oz) baby spinach leaves, chopped
2 slices grainy bread

1 Whisk together the eggs, milk, pepper, chives and dill in a small bowl.

2 Heat a large non-stick frying pan over medium heat. Add the egg mixture and cook for about 30 seconds, or until the eggs start to set around the edges. Using a wooden spatula, gently fold the eggs over, then repeat the folding process until the eggs are just cooked. The eggs should be quite soft.

3 Gently stir in the salmon and spinach until the salmon is heated through and the spinach is wilted. Serve the eggs on toasted grainy bread.

COOK'S TIP
One of the most important changes you can make to lower the GI of your diet is to choose a low GI bread. Choose a grainy bread, pumpernickel bread, sourdough or a stoneground wholemeal bread.

Ⓖ GI LOW

Per serve
1370 kJ (325 Cal), 13 g fat (saturated 3 g),
30 g protein, 21 g carbohydrate, 3 g fibre,
1228 mg sodium

FIELD MUSHROOMS WITH RICOTTA AND ROASTED TOMATOES SERVES 4

There's nothing quite like tomatoes that have ripened in the sunshine on the vine. The next best thing is to buy tomatoes still on the vine—you will find they have developed a fuller flavour. Preparation time: 10 minutes Cooking time: 15 minutes

250 g (9 oz) cherry tomatoes on the vine
1 tablespoon balsamic vinegar
2 tablespoons extra-virgin olive oil
freshly ground black pepper
juice of 1 lemon
1 tablespoon chopped dill
4 field or flat mushrooms, stems trimmed
100 g (3½ oz) low fat ricotta cheese
4 thick slices sourdough or grainy bread, to serve

1 Preheat the oven to 180°C (350°F/Gas 4). Put the tomatoes on a baking tray lined with baking paper. Drizzle with balsamic vinegar and 1 tablespoon of the oil and sprinkle with pepper. Bake for 8–10 minutes, or until the tomatoes are soft.

2 Combine the remaining oil, lemon juice and dill in a bowl and season with a little pepper. Brush the mushrooms generously with the oil marinade, then place, stem-side down, on a heated char-grill pan or frying pan and cook for 3 minutes. Turn the mushrooms over, crumble the ricotta over the top and spoon over the remaining marinade. Cook for a further 2–3 minutes, or until the mushrooms are soft.

3 Serve the mushrooms and roasted tomatoes with toasted sourdough or grainy bread.

ACTIVITY TIPS

If possible, walk to work, or at least part of the way, or walk the children to school.

Keep comfortable shoes at work so that you never have an excuse not to exercise.

GI LOW Ⓖ

Per serve
1015 kJ (240 Cal), 13 g fat (saturated 3 g),
9 g protein, 21 g carbohydrate, 4 g fibre,
272 mg sodium

TRADITIONAL SCOTTISH PORRIDGE SERVES 2

Many traditional Scottish meals are both rich in nutrients and low GI. Oatmeal was once a staple of Scotland, used not only to make porridge, but incorporated in baked goods and in many dishes as a thickener. If you have never tasted traditional porridge, give this recipe a try. And yes, Scottish porridge always uses black pepper. Soaking time: Overnight Cooking time: 10–15 minutes

125 g (4½ oz/1 cup) medium or coarse oatmeal
½ teaspoon salt
freshly ground black pepper
extra raw oatmeal, to serve
250 ml (9 fl oz/1 cup) low fat milk, to serve

1 The night before, combine the oatmeal, the salt, a generous sprinkle of pepper and 750 ml (26 fl oz/3 cups) water in a non-stick saucepan. Leave to soak overnight (there is no need to refrigerate, except in very hot weather).

2 In the morning, put the saucepan over medium heat, bring to the boil, then reduce the heat and simmer for 10 minutes, stirring occasionally.

3 Spoon the porridge into bowls and sprinkle with a little raw oatmeal. Traditionally, the steaming bowls of porridge are served with a small cup of milk on the side. Take half a spoonful of hot porridge, fill the rest of your spoon with the cold milk and enjoy.

COOK'S TIP
Search out oatmeal if you can, as it does taste infinitely better. You can find it in health-food stores and some supermarkets. Failing this, rolled oats are almost as good. (Rolled oats are simply steamed and flattened oats—the partial cooking of these reduces the flavour but does shorten the cooking time.) If you are using rolled oats, use 100 g (3½ oz/1 cup) oats and 625 ml (21 fl oz/2½ cups) water and reduce the cooking time to 3–5 minutes. There is no need to soak the rolled oats overnight.

GI LOW
Per serve
940 kJ (225 Cal), 5 g fat (saturated 1 g),
10 g protein, 40 g carbohydrate, 3 g fibre,
664 mg sodium

Recipe: Isobel McMillan

FRUITY QUINOA PORRIDGE SERVES 4

Quinoa (pronounced keen-wa) is a tiny, quick-cooking grain. It is rich in nutrients, has less than 5 per cent fat, with no saturated fat, and a low GI of 53. Quinoa has a mild, nutty flavour and a slightly chewy texture. Look for it in larger supermarkets or health-food stores.
Preparation time: 10 minutes   Cooking time: 15 minutes

200 g (7 oz/1 cup) quinoa
500 ml (17 fl oz/2 cups) skim milk
1 apple, chopped with skin on
40 g (1½ oz/⅓ cup) sultanas
1 cinnamon stick or ½ teaspoon ground cinnamon
1 tablespoon pure floral honey
125 ml (4 fl oz/½ cup) warm skim milk, extra, to serve

1 Put the quinoa in a sieve and rinse well under cold running water. Tip the quinoa into a saucepan, then pour in the milk. Bring to the boil, then reduce the heat and simmer for 5 minutes. Add the apple, sultanas and cinnamon and simmer for 5–6 minutes, or until all of the liquid is absorbed. Remove the cinnamon stick, if using.

2 Serve the quinoa porridge in small bowls. Drizzle the honey over the top and serve with the extra skim milk.

GI LOW Ⓖ
Per serve
1220 kJ (290 Cal), 3 g fat (saturated <1 g),
13 g protein, 54 g carbohydrate, 4 g fibre,
75 mg sodium

BREAKFAST FRUIT LOAF MAKES 12 SLICES

Although it is difficult to predict the GI of baked foods containing flour, we know that fruit loaves have a lower GI because some of the flour is replaced with dried fruit. This loaf is also packed with the fibre needed for a healthy digestive system.

Soaking time: 30 minutes Preparation time: 10 minutes Cooking time: 1–1¼ hours

50 g (1¾ oz/¾ cup) All-Bran® cereal
300 ml (10½ fl oz) skim milk
225 g (8 oz/1½ cups) wholemeal
self-raising flour
1 teaspoon baking powder
90 g (3 oz/¾ cup) sultanas
50 g (1¾ oz/⅔ cup) dried apricots,
cut into small dice
50 g (1¾ oz/¼ cup) pitted prunes,
cut into small dice
75 g (2½ oz/⅓ cup) dark muscovado sugar
4 tablespoons pure floral honey

1 Put the bran cereal in a bowl, pour over the milk and soak for 30 minutes. Preheat the oven to 180°C (350°F/Gas 4).

2 Sift the flour and baking powder into a bowl and stir in the bran cereal mixture, together with any bran left in the sieve. Stir in the dried fruit, sugar and honey and mix well.

3 Spoon the mixture into a non-stick 900 g (2 lb) loaf tin (or brush the tin with oil to prevent sticking) and level the top. Bake for 1–1¼ hours, or until the loaf is cooked and golden brown on top.

4 Allow the loaf to cool a little in the tin before turning it out onto a wire rack to cool completely. The loaf will store for several weeks if wrapped in foil and kept in an airtight container.

COOK'S TIP
Muscovado sugar, sometimes called Barbados sugar, is a very dark brown unrefined sugar. Light and dark muscovado sugars both contain molasses; the darker variety is stickier and has a stronger molasses flavour than the light. If you can't find muscovado, use a good-quality dark brown sugar.

Ⓖ GI LOW
Per slice
720 kJ (170 Cal), <1 g fat (saturated 0 g),
4 g protein, 38 g carbohydrate, 4 g fibre,
207 mg sodium

FRENCH TOAST WITH BERRY COMPOTE SERVES 4

Enjoy this berry compote using your favourite mix of fresh or frozen berries—strawberries, raspberries, blackberries, blueberries or boysenberries. Berries don't ripen once they're picked, so choose carefully—the deeply coloured ones tend to be the sweetest and have the most flavour. Preparation time: 5 minutes Cooking time: 15 minutes

200 g (7 oz/1 cup) mixed berries
2 eggs
2 tablespoons low fat milk
4 slices fruit-and-muesli bread or fruit loaf
2 tablespoons pure maple syrup

1 Put the berries in a small saucepan and gently heat until the berries are warm and have softened.

2 Meanwhile, break the eggs into a flat dish, add the milk and whisk with a fork to combine. Add the slices of fruit bread and coat well, on both sides, with the egg mixture.

3 Heat a non-stick frying pan over medium heat and dry-fry 2 slices of the eggy bread for about 3 minutes on each side, or until brown. Repeat with the remaining 2 slices. Cut the bread in half and serve topped with the warm berries and 2 teaspoons of the maple syrup drizzled over the top of each.

COOK'S TIP
Berries are best eaten as soon as possible after you have bought them. If you need to keep them for a day or two, here's how to minimise mould. Take them out of the container and place on a couple of layers of paper towel, cover loosely with plastic wrap and store in the refrigerator. Don't wash them until you're ready to use them.

GI LOW ⑤
Per serve
890 kJ (215 Cal), 4 g fat (saturated 1 g),
7 g protein, 37 g carbohydrate, 4 g fibre,
140 mg sodium

STRAWBERRY YOGHURT CRUNCH SERVES 4

Although nuts and seeds are high in fat, research shows that people who eat them often tend to be slimmer and healthier. This is because the fat in nuts and seeds is mainly unsaturated (the healthy kind of fat), we probably don't absorb all of it, and they are packed with other essential nutrients and fibre. Preparation time: 10 minutes Cooking time: 1–2 minutes

50 g (1¾ oz) mixed raw nuts, such as
cashews, peanuts, pistachios and almonds
15 g (½ oz) sunflower seeds
15 g (½ oz) pepitas (pumpkin seeds)
600 g (1 lb 5 oz) low fat natural yoghurt
1 large mango, sliced
200 g (7 oz/1⅓ cups) strawberries, sliced
4 teaspoons pure floral honey

1 Heat a non-stick frying pan over medium heat and add the raw nuts and seeds. Dry-fry them for 1–2 minutes, stirring continuously until browned (take care as the nuts will burn very quickly). Remove from the heat and, when cool enough to handle, roughly chop with a large knife.

2 Take four glasses and spoon a little yoghurt into the bottom of each one. Divide the mango slices between the glasses, top with another layer of yoghurt, then finish with a layer of sliced strawberries.

3 Drizzle the honey over the strawberries and sprinkle the toasted nut and seed mixture over the top.

G GI LOW
Per serve
1070 kJ (255 Cal), 11 g fat (saturated 1 g),
14 g protein, 24 g carbohydrate, 3 g fibre,
110 mg sodium

BUCKWHEAT PANCAKES WITH BERRIES SERVES 4

Buckwheat is not a cereal grain like wheat but is actually the seed of an annual that's related to sorrel and rhubarb. It has a nutty flavour and is ground into a gritty flour for making pancakes, muffins, cookies, cakes, Russian blinis and soba noodles.
Preparation time: 10 minutes Cooking time: 10–15 minutes

130 g (4½ oz/1 cup) buckwheat flour
35 g (1¼ oz/¼ cup) wholemeal flour
1½ teaspoons baking powder
2 tablespoons raw (demerara) sugar
2 eggs, lightly beaten
250 ml (9 fl oz/1 cup) buttermilk
1 teaspoon vanilla essence
olive oil spray
4 tablespoons low fat natural yoghurt
150 g (5¼ oz/1 cup) blueberries

1 Combine the flours, baking powder and sugar in a mixing bowl. Make a well in the centre and pour in the eggs, buttermilk and vanilla essence and whisk until smooth. Add a little more milk if the pancake batter is too thick.

2 Heat a frying pan over medium heat and lightly spray with olive oil. Pour 60 ml (2 fl oz/¼ cup) of the mixture into the pan and cook for 1–2 minutes each side, or until the pancake is golden and cooked. Repeat with the remaining mixture to make 8 pancakes in total.

3 Serve two pancakes per person. Top the pancakes with a spoonful of yoghurt and some blueberries.

ACTIVITY TIP
Buy a pedometer and wear it on your waistband everyday. Make it your goal to reach 10,000 steps on most days.

GI LOW G
Per serve (2 pancakes)
1058 kJ (252 Cal), 5 g fat (saturated 2 g),
11 g protein, 39 g carbohydrate, 5 g fibre,
160 mg sodium

POACHED EGGS AND BACON WITH SPICY TOMATO SALSA SERVES 4

Eggs and bacon might sound like an unlikely inclusion in a healthy cookbook but cooked in the right way and served with one or two vegetables provides a perfect balance of carbohydrates, protein and fat. Preparation time: 10 minutes Cooking time: 10 minutes

4 eggs, at room temperature
4 rashers bacon, fat trimmed
4 grainy English muffins, split
30 g (1 oz/1 cup) rocket leaves
coriander leaves, to garnish (optional)

SPICY TOMATO SALSA
2 vine-ripened tomatoes, seeded and finely diced
¼ red (Spanish) onion, finely diced
1 green chilli, seeds removed and finely diced
juice of ½ lime
pinch of sugar
1 tablespoon chopped coriander leaves

1 To make the spicy tomato salsa, combine all the ingredients in a small bowl and set side.

2 Bring a large saucepan or deep frying pan of water to a simmer. Crack the eggs and gently slip them, one at a time, into the simmering water. Cook for 3–4 minutes, or until the egg whites are opaque and the yolk is still quite soft (or until cooked to your liking). Carefully lift out the eggs with a slotted spoon and drain on paper towels.

3 Preheat the grill to high and cook the bacon until crisp. Meanwhile, toast the muffin halves.

4 To serve, layer the muffins with a handful of rocket leaves, the bacon and top with a poached egg and a spoonful of tomato salsa. Garnish with coriander, if desired.

COOK'S TIP
To minimise the spreading of the egg whites when poaching eggs, break the egg into a teacup, then gently slip the egg into the water. Some cooks also like to add a dash of vinegar or lemon juice to the water before they poach the eggs. This helps the egg white to set, but may also flavour the eggs slightly.

G GI LOW
Per serve
1130 kJ (270 Cal), 8 g fat (saturated 2 g),
23 g protein, 27 g carbohydrate, 5 g fibre,
1090 mg sodium

ORANGE BIRCHER MUESLI SERVES 2

Soaking time: Overnight Preparation time: 5 minutes

100 g (3½ oz/1 cup) rolled oats
30 g (1 oz/¼ cup) sultanas
250 ml (9 fl oz/1 cup) orange juice
1 apple, grated with skin on
2 tablespoons low fat natural yoghurt
40 g (1½ oz/¼ cup) blueberries
4 strawberries, sliced

1 The night before, place the oats, sultanas and orange juice in a bowl, cover and leave in the refrigerator overnight.

2 In the morning, add the grated apple and yoghurt and mix well. Serve in two bowls topped with the blueberries and sliced strawberries.

GI LOW Ⓖ

Per serve
1455 kJ (345 Cal), 4 g fat (saturated <1 g),
8 g protein, 68 g carbohydrate, 7 g fibre,
35 mg sodium

TOASTED MUESLI MAKES ABOUT 32 SERVES

Preparation time: 10 minutes Cooking time: 25–35 minutes

750 g (1 lb 10 oz/7½ cups) rolled oats
250 g (9 oz/2 cups) rye or barley flakes
(or use extra oats)
80 g (2¾ oz/½ cup) sesame seeds
125 g (4½ oz/1⅓ cups) flaked almonds
90 g (3 oz/1 cup) wheatgerm
200 g (7 oz/1½ cups) mixed dried fruit,
such as sultanas, peaches,
pears, apricots, apples
250 g (9 oz/2 cups) sultanas
75 g (2½ oz/½ cup) pepitas (pumpkin seeds)
125 g (4½ oz/1 cup) sunflower seeds

1 Preheat the oven to 180°C (350°F/Gas 4). Spread half the rolled oats and half the rye or barley flakes on a large ungreased baking tray. Bake for 10–15 minutes, stirring several times, until the oats are golden brown (take care they don't burn). Spread onto a large plate or tray to cool. Repeat with the remaining oats and rye or barley.

2 Put the sesame seeds and almonds on the tray and bake for 3 minutes, stirring occasionally, or until toasted and golden. Allow to cool.

3 Combine the toasted oats, rye, sesame seeds and almonds with the remaining ingredients and mix well. The toasted muesli will store for 1 month if kept in an airtight container.

GI LOW Ⓖ

Per 60 g (2 oz) serve
990 kJ (235 Cal), 10 g fat (saturated 1 g),
7 g protein, 30 g carbohydrate, 5 g fibre,
5 mg sodium

Recipe: Dr Rosemary Stanton

Left: Toasted muesli

MIXED BERRY MUFFINS MAKES 8–10

You will find unprocessed oat bran in the cereal section of your supermarket. It's soft and has quite a bland flavour but is very useful in baked goods, such as muffins, as a partial substitute for flour because it boosts the fibre and lowers the GI.

Soaking time: 10 minutes   Preparation time: 10 minutes   Cooking time: 15 minutes

35 g (1¼ oz/½ cup) All-Bran® cereal
125 ml (4 fl oz/½ cup) low fat milk
60 g (2 oz/½ cup) self-raising flour
2 teaspoons baking powder
½ teaspoon ground cinnamon
75 g (2½ oz/½ cup) unprocessed oat bran
150 g (5¼ oz/1 cup) blueberries
150 g (5¼ oz/1¼ cups) raspberries
1 egg, lightly beaten
2 tablespoons pure floral honey
½ teaspoon vanilla essence

1 Preheat the oven to 180°C (350°F/Gas 4). Line a 12-hole standard muffin tin with paper cases.

2 Put the bran cereal in a bowl, pour over the milk and soak for 10 minutes. Sift the flour, baking powder and cinnamon into a large bowl. Stir in the oat bran, then fold in the blueberries and raspberries. Combine the egg, honey and vanilla in a small bowl.

3 Add the egg mixture and bran cereal mixture to the dry ingredients and stir gently with a wooden spoon until just combined; do not overmix. Spoon the mixture into the prepared muffin holes and bake for about 15 minutes, or until lightly browned and a skewer inserted into the centre of a muffin comes out clean. Cool for 5 minutes in the tin before transferring to a wire rack.

G GI LOW
Per muffin
420 kJ (100 Cal), 1 g fat (saturated 0 g),
4 g protein, 19 g carbohydrate, 3 g fibre,
145 mg sodium

FRUIT COMPOTE SERVES 6

We often sweeten recipes with honey rather than sugar. Since every species of flower has a unique nectar, honey from different types of flowers can have very different flavours and qualities. The lower GI honeys tend to be pure floral honeys such as 'yellowbox' rather than a blended product. Preparation time: 10 minutes Cooking time: 10 minutes

750 ml (26 fl oz/3 cups) apple juice
1 tablespoon pure floral honey
1 cinnamon stick
8 cardamom pods
100 g (3½ oz/¾ cup) dried pear halves
100 g (3½ oz/1¼ cups) dried apples
100 g (3½ oz/½ cup) dried apricots
100 g (3½ oz/½ cup) prunes

1 Combine the apple juice, honey, cinnamon stick, cardamom pods, pears, apples and apricots in a saucepan. Bring to the boil, then reduce the heat and simmer for 10 minutes, or until the fruit has softened.

2 Remove the pan from the heat, add the prunes, then transfer to a serving dish and leave to cool. When cool, cover and refrigerate until ready to serve.

ACTIVITY TIP
People who exercise are happier—being active for just 20 minutes a day helps to lift your spirits and improve your mood.

GI LOW Ⓖ

Per serve
930 kJ (221 Cal), <1 g fat (saturated <1 g),
2 g protein, 52 g carbohydrate, 6 g fibre,
22 mg sodium

MUSTARD-ROASTED FRUITS MAKES 4 CUPS

These wonderful mustard-roasted fruits are like a hot, roasted, whole fruit chutney. All you need is a spoonful over a slice of lean ham off the bone, or serve with your favourite cold meats.

Preparation time: 10 minutes Cooking time: 30 minutes

160 g (5½ oz/1 cup) dried figs
150 g (5¼ oz/1 cup) dried figlets
150 g (5¼ oz/1 cup) dried pear halves
90 g (3 oz/½ cup) dried apricots
110 g (3¾ oz/½ cup) pitted prunes
1 tablespoon mustard powder
2 tablespoons yellow mustard seeds
½ teaspoon salt
230 g (8 oz/1 cup) soft brown sugar
125 ml (4 fl oz/½ cup) white wine vinegar
375 ml (13 fl oz/1½ cups) dry white wine

1 Preheat the oven to 200°C (400°F/Gas 6). Place the dried fruit in a roasting tin, sprinkle over the mustard powder, mustard seeds, salt and sugar. Add the vinegar and wine and stir gently to combine.

2 Roast in the oven, stirring and tossing occasionally, for about 30 minutes, or until the fruits caramelise (check them after 20–25 minutes). Add extra liquid if you prefer them a little moister. The fruits are preserved in vinegar and sugar so will last for 2 weeks if stored, covered, in a clean jar or plastic container in the refrigerator.

G GI LOW
Per serve (¼ cup)
680 kJ (160 Cal), trace fat (saturated 0 g),
1 g protein, 35 g carbohydrate, 6 g fibre,
110 mg sodium

Julie Le Clerc is the award-winning author of nine vibrant cookbooks. She was owner and chef of two successful cafés in New Zealand, had many years' experience in professional kitchens and boutique catering, worked as a private chef in homes around the world, and gained a reputation as an accomplished cooking demonstrator. These cooking experiences and a great love of travel continue to inspire and expand Julie's culinary repertoire. Returning to the Middle East for 3 months recently has increased her knowledge of, and affection for, the fascinating cuisine of these lands.

BERRY AND BANANA SMOOTHIE SERVES 2

Preparation time: 5 minutes

*100 g (3½ oz/½ cup) frozen berries,
such as raspberries, strawberries,
blueberries, or a mixture
1 banana, chopped
400 ml (14 fl oz) canned light (skim)
evaporated milk
2 scoops (50 g/1¾ oz) low fat frozen yoghurt
or low fat ice-cream*

1 Combine all the ingredients in a blender and blend until smooth. Pour into two tall glasses and serve with a straw.

GI LOW G

Per serve
680 kJ (160 Cal), 1 g fat (saturated 0 g),
10 g protein, 29 g carbohydrate, 5 g fibre,
100 mg sodium

CARROT, APPLE AND GINGER JUICE SERVES 4

Preparation time: 10 minutes

*2 carrots, peeled
2 apples, cored
560 ml (19 fl oz/2¼ cups) fresh orange juice
½ teaspoon finely grated ginger*

1 If you have a juicer, juice the carrots and apples into a jug. Mix in the orange juice and ginger. Alternatively, use a blender to blend the ingredients until as smooth as possible. Pour the juice into four glasses and serve with ice, if desired.

COOK'S TIP
It's easy to overdo the kilojoules (calories) when drinking fruit juice, so it is a good idea to mix a fruit with a vegetable, as we've done here. This cuts both the sweetness and the kilojoules, while providing many of the nutrients found in whole food.

GI LOW G

Per serve
380 kJ (90 Cal), 0 g fat (saturated 0 g),
1 g protein, 21 g carbohydrate, 3 g fibre,
23 mg sodium

Left: Berry and banana smoothie

LUNCHES AND LIGHT MEALS

ALTHOUGH LUNCH IS OFTEN EATEN ON THE RUN, IT IS IMPORTANT TO REFUEL 4 OR 5 HOURS AFTER BREAKFAST. IT DOESN'T NEED TO BE A BIG MEAL. IN FACT, IF YOU FIND YOURSELF FEELING SLEEPY IN THE AFTERNOON, IT MAY HELP TO KEEP IT LIGHT WITH PROTEIN, VEGETABLES AND A SMALL SERVE OF CARBS.

BRUSCHETTA MAKES 4 OF EACH

Bruschetta, an Italian speciality, is toasted bread seasoned with olive oil and garlic. It is made using a dense, often day-old bread. Make the basic bruschetta and then choose from one of the toppings below. There is enough of each topping for four slices of bruschetta.
Preparation time: 10 minutes each Cooking time: 2–5 minutes each

BASIC BRUSCHETTA
4 slices sourdough bread,
cut on the diagonal
olive oil spray
1 garlic clove, halved

TOMATO AND BASIL
3 vine-ripened tomatoes, finely chopped
1 garlic clove, crushed
½ red (Spanish) onion, finely chopped
2 tablespoons finely shredded basil
2 teaspoons extra-virgin olive oil
2 teaspoons balsamic vinegar
freshly ground black pepper

RICOTTA AND ASPARAGUS
100 g (3½ oz) reduced fat ricotta cheese
1 tablespoon basil pesto
175 g (6 oz/1 bunch) asparagus, trimmed
freshly ground black pepper

HARICOT BEAN AND OLIVE
400 g (14 oz) can haricot beans,
rinsed and drained
juice of ½ lemon
2 teaspoons olive oil
freshly ground black pepper
2 tablespoons chopped kalamata olives
4 thyme sprigs, to garnish

1 To make the basic bruschetta, spray the sourdough slices on both sides with olive oil and toast under a grill or in a char-grill pan until golden. Rub the cut garlic cloves over each slice of toast.

2 To make the tomato and basil topping, combine the tomatoes, garlic, onion, basil, oil and balsamic vinegar in a bowl. Season with pepper, then spoon the tomato mixture onto the bruschetta.

3 To make the ricotta and asparagus topping, combine the ricotta cheese and pesto in a small bowl. Heat a char-grill pan over medium heat, spray the asparagus with olive oil and cook for 2–3 minutes, or until tender. Cut the asparagus into pieces. Spread the bruschetta with the ricotta mixture, top with asparagus pieces and season with pepper.

4 To make the haricot bean and olive topping, put the beans, lemon juice and oil in the bowl of a food processor, season with pepper, then blend to a smooth purée—adding more lemon juice for a creamier texture, if desired. Spread the bean mixture over the bruschetta, top with the olives and garnish with a sprig of thyme.

Ⓖ GI LOW
Per slice (tomato and basil)
450 kJ (110 Cal), 3 g fat (saturated 0 g),
4 g protein, 16 g carbohydrate, 3 g fibre,
158 mg sodium

Ⓖ GI LOW
Per slice (ricotta and asparagus)
530 kJ (125 Cal), 5 g fat (saturated 2 g),
6 g protein, 13 g carbohydrate, 5 g fibre,
244 mg sodium

Ⓖ GI LOW
Per slice (haricot bean and olive)
415 kJ (100 Cal), 3 g fat (saturated <1 g),
4 g protein, 12 g carbohydrate, 4 g fibre,
285 mg sodium

CRUMBED CHICKEN ON ROAST SWEET POTATO SALAD SERVES 2

Crumbed pieces of tender chicken, layered on a tasty potato salad and drizzled with a creamy honey mustard dressing—the perfect dish for a lunch or light meal. Preparation time: 20 minutes Cooking time: 25 minutes

ROAST SWEET POTATO SALAD
1 tablespoon olive oil
2 tablespoons balsamic vinegar
3 teaspoons soft brown sugar
1 orange sweet potato (about 300 g/10½ oz), cut into 5 mm (¼ in) thick slices
mixed green salad leaves, to serve
1 tablespoon chopped basil, to garnish

CRUMBED CHICKEN
2 tablespoons low fat natural yoghurt
2 tablespoons low fat milk
85 g (3 oz/1 cup) dry wholegrain breadcrumbs (see tip)
½ teaspoon paprika
freshly ground black pepper
300 g (10½ oz) skinless chicken breast or thigh fillets, trimmed and cut in half

HONEY MUSTARD DRESSING
1 tablespoon Dijon mustard
1 tablespoon tomato sauce (ketchup)
2 teaspoons lemon juice
2 tablespoons low fat natural yoghurt
1 teaspoon pure floral honey

1 Preheat the oven to 220°C (425°F/Gas 7). To make the roast sweet potato salad, combine the oil, vinegar and brown sugar in a large bowl. Add the sweet potato and toss to coat in the oil. Transfer to a shallow baking tray and roast for 25 minutes, or until soft and starting to brown. Remove from the oven and leave for 10 minutes to cool a little. (Note: If you prepare the sweet potato and the crumbed chicken at the same time, they can then go in the oven together.)

2 To make the crumbed chicken, put the yoghurt in a flat dish or bowl and stir in the milk to thin it a little. Combine the breadcrumbs and paprika in a bowl and season with pepper. Dip the chicken into the yoghurt, allow the excess to drain off, then coat in the breadcrumbs. Put the crumbed chicken on a baking tray lined with baking paper and bake for 20 minutes, or until the chicken is golden brown and cooked through. Remove and slice into strips on the diagonal.

3 To make the honey mustard dressing, put all the ingredients into a small bowl and stir to combine.

4 To serve, lay the salad leaves on a plate, top with slices of roasted sweet potato, a few more salad leaves, then more sweet potato. Lay the crumbed chicken on top of the salad and drizzle with the honey mustard dressing. Scatter over the basil.

COOK'S TIP

To make the dry wholegrain breadcrumbs, take 4 slices of low GI wholegrain bread and break into small pieces. Spread out on a baking tray and bake in a 220°C (425°F/Gas 7) oven for 5 minutes, or until golden brown. Cool slightly, then transfer to the bowl of a food processor and process to make small crumbs.

GI LOW G
Per serve
2495 kJ (595 Cal), 19 g fat (saturated 4 g),
44 g protein, 58 g carbohydrate, 6 g fibre,
594 mg sodium

QUINOA TABBOULI WITH PRAWNS SERVES 4

Quinoa is one of those versatile grains that you can make a meal of throughout the day—and it has a low GI of 53. This version of tabbouli uses quinoa instead of bulgur wheat and is made with pistachios. The fresh, strong flavours of lime and basil complement the prawns beautifully. Marinating time: 30 minutes Preparation time: 15 minutes Cooking time: 15 minutes

24 raw king prawns, peeled and deveined, with tails intact
zest and juice of 1 lemon
1 teaspoon ground cumin
2 green chillies, finely diced
125 g (4½ oz/½ cup) low fat natural yoghurt, to serve

PISTACHIO TABBOULI
200 g (7 oz/1 cup) quinoa, rinsed well
1 tablespoon olive oil
1 teaspoon ground cumin
freshly ground black pepper
75 g (2½ oz/½ cup) pistachio nuts, roughly chopped
½ red (Spanish) onion, finely diced
1 tomato, diced
30 g (1 oz/½ cup) chopped basil
juice of 1 lime

1 Put the prawns, lemon zest and juice, cumin and chillies in a non-metallic bowl. Mix well to coat the prawns in the marinade. Refrigerate the prawns for 30 minutes to allow the flavours to develop.

2 To make the pistachio tabbouli, put the rinsed quinoa in a saucepan and cover with 500 ml (17 fl oz/2 cups) water. Bring to the boil, then reduce the heat and simmer for about 10 minutes, or until the grains are tender and translucent. While still warm, transfer to a bowl and add the remaining ingredients. Mix well and set aside.

3 Soak 8 bamboo skewers for 30 minutes. Thread 3 prawns onto each skewer and cook on a heated barbecue or in a char-grill pan for 2 minutes each side, or until pink and cooked through. Spoon the tabbouli onto plates, top with two skewers per plate, and drizzle with the yoghurt.

COOK'S TIP
As a variation, use almonds or cashews instead of the pistachio nuts, or substitute mint leaves for the basil.

GI LOW
Per serve
1755 kJ (420 Cal), 15 g fat (saturated 2 g),
34 g protein, 35 g carbohydrate, 5 g fibre,
845 mg sodium

LENTIL BRUSCHETTA SERVES 8

This red lentil spread makes a delicious topping for bruschetta, or you could use it as a sandwich spread or a dip for fresh vegetables. Serve with a green salad, if desired.

Preparation time: 15 minutes Cooking time: 20 minutes

250 g (9 oz/1 cup) red lentils
1 bay leaf
3 tablespoons olive oil
1 garlic clove, crushed
1 large red capsicum (pepper), finely chopped
1 tablespoon paprika
1 loaf (640 g/1 lb 7 oz) sliced
sourdough bread (about 16 slices)
50 g (1³/₄ oz/¹/₂ cup) grated strong cheese,
such as Romano

1 Rinse the lentils and place them in a large saucepan. Cover with plenty of water and add the bay leaf. Bring to the boil, then reduce the heat and simmer for about 15 minutes, or until the lentils are very soft, skimming off any foam as they cook. Drain and remove the bay leaf.

2 Heat the oil in a frying pan and sauté the garlic and capsicum for about 5 minutes, or until soft. Stir in the paprika, then remove from the heat. Mix in the lentils. (For a smooth spread, purée the mixture in a food processor.)

3 Spread the lentils onto slices of toasted sourdough, sprinkle with the cheese and place under a hot grill until the cheese has melted. Serve immediately. You may like to serve this with a green salad.

ACTIVITY TIP
Use half an hour of your lunch break to get outside and take a walk around the block. This is an easy way to fit regular exercise into a busy work schedule.

GI LOW Ⓖ
Per serve (2 slices bread)
1510 kJ (360 Cal), 12 g fat (saturated 3 g),
15 g protein, 46 g carbohydrate, 7 g fibre,
510 mg sodium

Recipe from: Passion for Pulses

CHACHOUKA SERVES 4

Chachouka, eggs served in a tangy mixture of tomatoes, capsicums (peppers)—red, yellow and green—and chillies, is enjoyed throughout the Middle East. Serve as a brunch or light meal with chunky grainy toast.

Preparation time: 15 minutes Cooking time: 25–35 minutes

1 tablespoon olive oil
1 small red capsicum (pepper),
seeded and thinly sliced
1 small yellow capsicum (pepper),
seeded and thinly sliced
1 small green capsicum (pepper),
seeded and thinly sliced
2 garlic cloves, finely chopped
1–2 small red chillies, seeded and
finely chopped
400 g (14 oz) can Italian peeled
tomatoes, chopped
1 teaspoon harissa (page 162,
or ready-made)
1 teaspoon caraway seeds, ground
½ teaspoon sweet paprika
½ teaspoon ground cumin
4 large eggs
2 tablespoons chopped chives or flat-leaf
(Italian) parsley
4 thick slices grainy bread

1 Heat the oil in a large frying pan over low heat and gently cook the capsicums for about 10 minutes, or until soft. Stir in the garlic and chilli and cook for a further 1–2 minutes. Add the tomatoes, harissa and spices and stir to combine well. Increase the heat to medium and let the tomato mixture cook, uncovered, for 10–15 minutes, or until the tomatoes have reduced to a thick pulp.

2 Using the back of a spoon, make four equally spaced depressions in the tomato mixture, then carefully break one egg into each depression. Cover and leave to simmer for about 5 minutes, or until the whites are just cooked but the yolks are still soft. Sprinkle with the chives or parsley and serve immediately with toasted grainy bread.

3 As an alternative cooking method, pour the tomato mixture into four individual ovenproof dishes. Make a slight depression in the top of the tomato mixture in each dish, then break one egg into each depression. Cover lightly with foil and bake in a preheated 180°C (350°F/Gas 4) oven for 15–20 minutes, or until the eggs are set. Take care when serving, as the dishes will be hot.

G GI LOW

Per serve
1105 kJ (265 Cal), 11 g fat (saturated 2 g),
13 g protein, 26 g carbohydrate, 5 g fibre,
375 mg sodium

Recipe: Liz and Ian Hemphill, Herbies Spices

VEGETABLE CHILLI BOWL SERVES 4–6

This vegetable variation of chilli con carne has a lively spicy taste and is a complete meal in a bowl. Vegetarians will love this chunky chilli dish and meat eaters won't even notice that the meat is missing.

Preparation time: 15 minutes Cooking time: 20 minutes

2 tablespoons olive oil
2 onions, roughly chopped
3 garlic cloves, finely chopped
2 red capsicums (peppers), halved and cut into squares
2 zucchini (courgettes), cut into chunks
1 tablespoon chilli powder, or to taste
1 tablespoon ground cumin
2 x 400 g (14 oz) cans peeled tomatoes, roughly chopped, juice reserved
440 g (15½ oz) can red kidney beans, rinsed and drained
440 g (15½ oz) can chickpeas, rinsed and drained
¼ teaspoon salt
freshly ground black pepper
15 g (½ oz/½ cup) chopped flat-leaf (Italian) parsley
25 g (1 oz/½ cup) chopped coriander leaves
2 tablespoons lemon juice

1 Heat the oil in a flameproof casserole dish over medium heat. Add the onions, garlic and capsicums and cook for 5 minutes, then add the zucchini and cook for a further 3 minutes.

2 Add the chilli powder and cumin and stir for a minute to combine, then add the chopped tomatoes with their juice, the drained kidney beans and chickpeas. Season with the salt and plenty of pepper. Cover and cook over low heat for 8–10 minutes, or until the zucchini is tender. Stir in the parsley, coriander and lemon juice.

3 If preferred, you may like to serve this with separate bowls of grated cheddar cheese and yoghurt for everyone to help themselves, plus some crusty low GI bread, such as sourdough, to mop up the juices.

Margaret Fulton is one of Australia's leading cookery writers. Through her interest in food and nutrition, Margaret is a Governor (Honorary) of the University of Sydney Nutrition Research Foundation. Concerned for our future food supplies, Margaret has taken a stand against genetically modified food. She launched the *True Food Guide*, a Greenpeace book that advises shoppers on GE-free foods. Her pre-eminence in the food world was given official recognition when she was awarded the OAM (Medal of the Order of Australia) in the Queen's Birthday Honours of 1993. Margaret was made a National Living Treasure in 1998.

GI LOW ⒢
Per serve (6)
900 kJ (215 Cal), 8 g fat (saturated 1 g),
9 g protein, 22 g carbohydrate, 9 g fibre,
465 mg sodium

POTATO AND SWEET CORN FRITTATA SERVES 4

Frittata is one of the easiest meals to prepare when you want to make do with what's in the pantry and refrigerator. Virtually any combination of vegetables is possible. Here we use new potatoes, onion and sweet corn, but peas and a little bacon are nice additions, if preferred. Preparation time: 20 minutes Cooking time: 20 minutes

1 tablespoon olive oil
1 onion, diced
1 garlic clove, crushed
440 g (15½ oz) can new potatoes, drained and diced
310 g (11 oz) can sweet corn kernels, drained
6 eggs
80 ml (2½ fl oz/⅓ cup) low fat milk
1 tablespoon chopped parsley
freshly ground black pepper

VEGETABLE SALAD
200 g (7 oz) sugar snap peas or snow peas (mangetout), trimmed
200 g (7 oz) asparagus, trimmed, cut into 3 cm (1¼ in) lengths
200 g (7 oz) broccoli, broken into small florets
2 tablespoons lemon juice
1 tablespoon olive oil

1 Heat half the oil in a large non-stick frying pan over medium heat. Add the onion and garlic and cook for 3 minutes, or until the onion is translucent. Add the potatoes and corn kernels to the pan and cook for 1–2 minutes to heat through, then transfer the vegetables to a bowl.

2 Break the eggs into another bowl, add the milk and parsley, season with pepper and beat lightly with a fork until combined.

3 Add the remaining oil to the frying pan, swirling the oil around to coat the base of the pan. Add the vegetables to the pan, spreading them out, then pour the egg mixture evenly over the vegetables. Cover and cook over medium–low heat for 10 minutes, or until the egg mixture is partially set. Place under a hot grill until the frittata is golden brown and puffed on top.

4 To make the vegetable salad, bring a large saucepan of water to the boil. Add the snap peas, asparagus and broccoli and boil for 2–3 minutes, or until the vegetables are bright green and just tender. Drain, rinse under cold water and refrigerate.

5 To make a salad dressing, put the lemon juice and oil in a screw-top jar and shake to combine. Serve the frittata in wedges with the salad and drizzle with the dressing.

G GI LOW
Per serve
1360 kJ (325 Cal), 13 g fat (saturated 3 g),
20 g protein, 31 g carbohydrate, 8 g fibre,
536 mg sodium

BEEFBURGERS WITH SALSA SERVES 4

Most beefburgers are made using hamburger mince, which is quite fatty (the fat makes them moist). Using minced rump steak with all the fat trimmed off (ask your butcher to mince it for you) may make this burger a little drier, but with the delicious tomato and bean salsa you won't notice the difference. Preparation time: 15 minutes Cooking time: 1 hour 10 minutes

500 g (1 lb 2 oz) premium lean minced beef
½ onion, finely chopped
10 g (¼ oz/½ cup) flat-leaf (Italian) parsley, finely chopped
freshly ground black pepper
1 tablespoon olive oil

TOMATO AND BEAN SALSA
1 tablespoon olive oil
1 small onion, finely chopped
1 small red chilli, seeded and finely chopped
3 garlic cloves, crushed
1 teaspoon ground cumin
½ teaspoon sweet paprika
2 x 400 g (14 oz) cans Roma (plum) tomatoes
400 g (14 oz) can red kidney beans, drained
3 tablespoons chopped flat-leaf (Italian) parsley

1 To make the tomato and bean salsa, heat the oil in a saucepan over medium heat, then add the onion and chilli and cook for 5 minutes, or until the onion is soft. Add the garlic, cumin and paprika and cook for a further 2 minutes. Break the tomatoes into chunks in a bowl, then add them to the pan. Bring to the boil, then reduce the heat and simmer for 30 minutes. Add the kidney beans, return to the boil, then reduce the heat and simmer for a further 20 minutes. Stir in the parsley.

2 To make the beefburgers, combine the minced beef with the onion and parsley and season with pepper. Shape the mixture into four flat rounds, pressing firmly into shape. Brush each with a little oil, then cook on a heated barbecue or char-grill pan for 3–6 minutes on each side, turning once, until golden brown and cooked through. Serve the beefburgers with the salsa, and with a green salad, if desired.

GI LOW G
Per serve
1600 kJ (380 Cal), 19 g fat (saturated 5 g),
32 g protein, 18 g carbohydrate, 8 g fibre,
430 mg sodium

Recipe: Judy Davie, The Food Coach

PARSLEY, BUTTER BEAN AND CHERRY TOMATO STEW SERVES 4

This quick and easy stew makes a simple side dish to serve with meat or chicken, or enjoy as a light meal in itself. Top with pitted black olives if you wish. Preparation time: 20 minutes Cooking time: 15 minutes

1 tablespoon olive oil
1 red (Spanish) onion, chopped
1 red capsicum (pepper), thinly sliced
1 yellow capsicum (pepper), thinly sliced
2 garlic cloves, chopped (or more to taste)
2.5 cm (1 in) piece ginger, grated
pinch of saffron threads
250 g (9 oz/1½ cups) cherry tomatoes, halved
½ teaspoon sugar
2 x 400 g (14 oz) cans butter beans, rinsed and drained
½ teaspoon ground cinnamon
1 teaspoon paprika
freshly ground black pepper
50 g (1¾ oz/½ small bunch) flat-leaf (Italian) parsley, roughly chopped
pita bread, warmed and sliced, to serve (optional)

1 Heat the oil in a large frying pan over medium heat. Add the onion, capsicums, garlic and ginger and cook for 10 minutes, or until the onions are golden and soft. Stir in the saffron threads, then the tomatoes and sugar and cook for a further 5 minutes.

2 When the tomatoes are heated through, add the butter beans, cinnamon and paprika. Stir gently. Season with pepper and sprinkle over the parsley. Serve with pita bread for mopping up the juices, if desired.

ACTIVITY TIP
Gardening and DIY are great ways to be more active at home when weather permits. Otherwise, do some spring cleaning around the house for a total body workout.

GI LOW
Per serve
405 kJ (95 Cal), 5 g fat (saturated <1 g),
5 g protein, 8 g carbohydrate, 5 g fibre,
14 mg sodium

CHERMOULA CHICKPEA BURGERS SERVES 4

Chermoula gives these chickpea burgers a tangy Moroccan flavour. Chermoula combines the robust flavours of cumin, paprika and turmeric with onion, parsley and coriander, plus a hint of garlic and cayenne pepper.

Preparation time: 20 minutes Marinating time: 20 minutes Cooking time: 15 minutes

CHICKPEA BURGERS
1 tablespoon extra-virgin olive oil
1 large onion, finely chopped
1 garlic clove, crushed
400 g (14 oz) can chickpeas, rinsed and drained
85 g (3 oz/1 cup loosely packed) fresh wholegrain breadcrumbs
1 egg, lightly beaten
freshly ground black pepper
1–2 tablespoons chickpea (besan) flour, to thicken (optional)
2 tablespoons chermoula spice mix (page 162, or ready-made)
1 teaspoon olive oil

pita bread, warmed and cut into quarters
cos lettuce leaves
hommous (page 163, or ready-made)
tabbouli (page 163, or ready-made)
baked beetroot salad (page 164) or ready-made beetroot dip

1 To make the chickpea burgers, heat the oil in a frying pan, add the onion and garlic and cook over low heat for 5 minutes, or until golden. Put the chickpeas in a food processor and purée until they resemble breadcrumbs. Add the fresh breadcrumbs and egg and season with pepper, then add the onion and garlic and process for a few seconds, or until the ingredients are just combined. Add 1–2 tablespoons chickpea flour if the mixture is too wet.

2 Use 1 heaped tablespoon of the mixture to form each burger (the mixture will make 8 burgers in total). Mix the chermoula with 2 tablespoons water. Brush the burgers generously with the chermoula, then leave to marinate for 20 minutes or so.

3 Heat the olive oil in a non-stick frying pan or on the barbecue hotplate and cook the chickpea burgers over medium heat for 4–5 minutes each side, or until browned. Don't have the heat too high or they will burn, which will spoil the flavour.

4 Serve the chickpea burgers with pita bread and lettuce, and separate bowls of hommous, tabbouli and baked beetroot salad or beetroot dip, and assemble the burgers at the table.

GI LOW G
Per serve (2 burgers)
925 kJ (220 Cal), 9 g fat (saturated 1 g),
9 g protein, 24 g carbohydrate, 5 g fibre,
296 mg sodium

SWEET POTATO CAKES WITH ROAST TOMATO SALAD SERVES 2

Don't hold back on the tomato salad with your sweet potato cakes. Tomatoes are an almost exclusive source of the anti-oxidant lycopene, associated with a reduced risk of some cancers. Preparation time: 25 minutes Cooking time: 45 minutes

SWEET POTATO CAKES
1 large potato (about 300 g/10½ oz), roughly chopped
1 orange sweet potato (about 300 g/10½ oz), roughly chopped
olive oil spray
2 rashers bacon, fat trimmed, diced
100 g (3½ oz/1 cup) rolled oats
2 tablespoons chopped parsley
freshly ground black pepper

ROAST TOMATO SALAD
3 Roma (plum) tomatoes, halved lengthways
1 garlic clove, crushed
2 teaspoons olive oil
freshly ground black pepper
40 g (1½ oz) baby spinach leaves

HERB MAYONNAISE
1 tablespoon mayonnaise
1 tablespoon low fat natural yoghurt
2 teaspoons finely chopped chives
1 tablespoon shredded basil

1 Preheat the oven to 200°C (400°F/Gas 6). To make the roast tomato salad, place the tomatoes, cut-side up, on a baking tray. Smear the cut side of the tomatoes with the garlic, drizzle over the oil and season with pepper. Bake for 30 minutes, or until soft.

2 Meanwhile, to make the sweet potato cakes, cook the potato and sweet potato in a large saucepan of boiling water for 10 minutes, or until soft.

3 Spray a non-stick frying pan with olive oil and cook the bacon over medium heat until browned. Put the oats into the bowl of a food processor and process briefly until the oats resemble coarse breadcrumbs.

4 Drain the cooked potato and sweet potato and mash them. Add the bacon, oats and parsley and season with pepper. When cool enough to handle, shape the potato mixture into four flat rounds.

5 Reheat the frying pan over medium heat, spray with olive oil and cook the sweet potato cakes for 2–3 minutes on each side, or until browned.

6 To make the herb mayonnaise, combine all the ingredients in a bowl.

7 To serve, place two sweet potato cakes on each plate and top with a few spinach leaves, three tomato halves and a dollop of mayonnaise.

GI LOW

Per serve
1160 kJ (275 Cal), 7 g fat (saturated 1 g),
11 g protein, 38 g carbohydrate, 7 g fibre,
235 mg sodium

TUSCAN-STYLE BEANS WITH TOMATOES AND SAGE SERVES 4

Tuscan beans can be served as a course on their own—either hot or cold—or as an accompaniment to meat dishes. Provide plenty of crusty sourdough bread to mop up the juices. Preparation time: 15 minutes Cooking time: 25 minutes

125 g (4½ oz/1 cup) shelled fresh (or frozen) broad beans
2 teaspoons extra-virgin olive oil
2 garlic cloves, finely chopped
400 g (14 oz) can Italian chopped tomatoes, or tomato pieces
400 g (14 oz) can cannellini beans, rinsed and drained
1½ teaspoons finely chopped sage or ½ teaspoon dried sage
freshly ground black pepper

1 Bring a saucepan of water to the boil and blanch the beans in boiling water for 3 minutes. Drain and refresh under cold running water. Peel the outer skins from the beans when they are cool enough to handle.

2 Heat the oil in a saucepan over low heat and cook the garlic for about 2 minutes. Add the tomatoes, cannellini beans and sage and simmer, covered, for 10 minutes. Stir in the broad beans and cook gently for a further 5–10 minutes, or until tender. Season with pepper.

COOK'S TIP
Sage has a lovely fresh aroma and flavour but it is quite intense. Use only 2 or 3 leaves so as not to overpower the other flavours in the dish. Dried sage (and dried herbs in general) has a more intense, concentrated flavour than fresh sage, so you only need to use about half the amount.

GI LOW Ⓖ
Per serve
579 kJ (138 Cal), 3 g fat (saturated <1 g),
8 g protein, 16 g carbohydrate, 7 g fibre,
283 mg sodium

NASI GORENG SERVES 4

Nasi goreng—Indonesian-style fried rice—is great as a light lunch using leftover cooked rice from the night before. Make sure you use one of the lower GI rices such as basmati or Doongara.

Preparation time: 10 minutes Cooking time: 10–15 minutes

4 eggs, at room temperature
1 egg, lightly beaten
1 teaspoon peanut oil
1 large onion, finely chopped
2 garlic cloves, crushed
1 tablespoon grated ginger
700 g (1 lb 9 oz/4 cups) cooked basmati or Doongara rice
1 tablespoon oyster sauce
2 tablespoons soy sauce
chopped parsley or spring onions, to serve

1 Bring a large saucepan or deep frying pan of water to a simmer and carefully crack the eggs and gently slip them, one at a time, into the simmering water. Poach for 3–4 minutes, or until the eggs are cooked to your liking. Lift out with a slotted spoon and drain on paper towels.

2 Heat a non-stick frying pan over medium heat, add the beaten egg and stir-fry until the egg is scrambled. Remove and set aside.

3 Heat the oil in the pan, add the onion, garlic and ginger and lightly fry for 3–5 minutes, or until the onion is soft. Add the cooked rice and toss well. Pour in the oyster sauce and soy sauce and toss to coat the rice in the sauces. Stir in the scrambled egg.

4 Spoon the rice into four bowls or plates and top each with a poached egg. Sprinkle with chopped parsley or spring onions.

COOK'S TIPS

To obtain 700 g (1 lb 9 oz/4 cups) cooked rice you will need 250 g (9 oz/1⅓ cups) raw rice.

The GI of rice varies according to the variety and its proportion of the slower digested amylose starch.

GI MEDIUM
Per serve
1530 kJ (365 Cal), 8 g fat (saturated 2 g),
14 g protein, 58 g carbohydrate, 2 g fibre,
1245 mg sodium

Recipe: Jill McMillan

SUSHI ROLLS MAKES 4 ROLLS

The low GI of sushi rolls is due to the special Japanese rice called koshihikari and the addition of rice vinegar. Add to this the nutrient-rich fish and you have a perfect light lunch that will keep the hunger pangs at bay all afternoon.

Preparation time: 20 minutes Standing time: 10 minutes Cooking time: 15 minutes

220 g (7¾ oz/1 cup) sushi rice (koshihikari rice)
60 ml (2 fl oz/¼ cup) Japanese rice vinegar
1 tablespoon caster sugar
4 sheets nori, toasted

SALMON FILLING
50 g (1¾ oz) smoked salmon, sliced
½ avocado, thinly sliced

TUNA FILLING
105 g (3½ oz) can tuna in water, drained
1 tablespoon low fat mayonnaise
½ Lebanese (short) cucumber, seeds removed, cut into long strips

1 Cook the rice in a large saucepan of boiling water for 13–15 minutes, or until the rice is tender. Drain the rice, without rinsing it, and place in a large bowl. Add the rice vinegar and sugar and stir into the rice. Cover with plastic wrap and leave to cool for about 10 minutes.

2 Run a bamboo sushi mat under water and shake off the excess water. Place one nori sheet on the sushi mat, rough side up and with the long end of the sheet closest to you. Using wet hands, place a quarter of the rice on the nori sheet, pat down the rice to cover the sheet, leaving 4 cm (1½ in) at the top of the sheet. Press the rice firmly onto the sheet and make a slight indent in the rice 4 cm (1½ in) from the bottom of the sheet, closest to you.

3 To make the salmon-filled rolls, place half the smoked salmon and half the avocado in the indent along the rice. Using the bamboo mat, firmly roll up the sushi. Remove the mat. Using a wet knife, cut the roll into thick slices. Repeat to make the second roll.

4 To make the tuna-filled rolls, combine the tuna with the mayonnaise. Place half the cucumber strips and half the tuna in the indent along the rice and roll up the sushi. Repeat to make the second roll.

5 You may like to serve the sushi rolls with accompaniments such as soy sauce for dipping (mix a little wasabi into the soy sauce for extra flavour) and pickled ginger.

GI LOW ⓖ
Per salmon roll
1320 kJ (315 Cal), 9 g fat (saturated 1 g),
11 g protein, 49 g carbohydrate, 6 g fibre,
530 mg sodium

GI LOW ⓖ
Per tuna roll
1190 kJ (280 Cal), 3 g fat (saturated <1 g),
16 g protein, 47 g carbohydrate, 3 g fibre,
220 mg sodium

SOUPS AND SALADS

SOUPS AND SALADS MAKE GREAT STARTERS,
ESPECIALLY WHEN YOU WANT TO LOSE WEIGHT.
THE EVIDENCE IS IN—WE KNOW THAT EATING
A MIXED SALAD TOSSED IN A VINAIGRETTE
DRESSING OR SIPPING A BOWL OF VEGETABLE
SOUP BEFORE A MAIN MEAL WILL HELP TO FILL
YOU UP SO THAT YOU WILL EAT LESS OVERALL.

MINESTRONE SERVES 4

Minestrone is absolutely delicious as a warming, hearty winter meal. And it is worth the little extra effort and time it takes to make as this quantity will generously serve four for a main meal or six as a starter and still leave leftovers for lunch. Leave out the bacon if you want a vegetarian meal. Preparation time: 20 minutes Cooking time: 50–55 minutes

1 tablespoon olive oil
1 large onion, finely chopped
1 leek, thinly sliced
2 garlic cloves, finely chopped
2 lean rashers bacon, chopped
2 carrots, sliced into 5 mm (1/4 in) rounds, or diced
2 celery sticks, thinly sliced
400 g (14 oz) can Italian chopped tomatoes or tomato pieces
1 bay leaf
1.5 litres (52 fl oz/6 cups) good-quality chicken, beef or vegetable stock
100 g (3 1/2 oz/1/2 cup) small pasta pieces or risoni
400 g (14 oz) can borlotti or cannellini beans, rinsed and drained
155 g (5 1/2 oz/1 cup) fresh or frozen peas
75 g (2 1/2 oz/1 cup) finely shredded cabbage
freshly ground black pepper
basil pesto or sun-dried tomato pesto, to serve (optional)
shaved Parmesan cheese, to serve (optional)

1 Heat the oil in a large heavy-based soup saucepan over medium heat. Add the onion, leek and garlic and cook for about 5 minutes, or until the onion is golden and soft. Add the bacon and cook for 1–2 minutes, then add the carrots, celery, tomatoes and bay leaf. Pour in 1.25 litres (44 fl oz/ 5 cups) of the stock and bring to the boil, then reduce the heat and simmer, covered, for 30 minutes.

2 Stir in the pasta and continue to simmer for 10–15 minutes, or until the pasta is al dente. Add more stock if the mixture is too thick.

3 Add the beans, peas and cabbage, season with pepper, then stir to combine and cook for a few minutes to heat the vegetables through.

4 Serve with a dollop of basil or sun-dried tomato pesto and scatter over the Parmesan cheese, if using. You may like to serve with sourdough bread to mop up the juices.

COOK'S TIP
To freeze, cool the soup to room temperature and divide among single serve plastic containers with lids. Label with the recipe name and date using an indelible marker.

G GI LOW
Per serve
1030 kJ (245 Cal), 7 g fat (saturated 2 g),
13 g protein, 27 g carbohydrate, 9 g fibre,
1585 mg sodium

PAN-FRIED LAMB SALAD WITH TZATZIKI SERVES 4

Tzatziki is a traditional Greek cucumber and yoghurt dip and makes a delicious dressing for this lamb salad. It is often served as a dip with dolmades or vegetable platters. You can find ready-made tzatziki in the refrigerated cabinet section of the supermarket.
Preparation time: 20 minutes Cooking time: 10 minutes

olive oil spray
500 g (1 lb 2 oz) lamb backstraps
(or lean fillets)
freshly ground black pepper
60 g (2 oz/2 cups) rocket leaves
60 g (2 oz/2 cups) baby spinach leaves
160 g (5½ oz/1 cup) cherry tomatoes,
halved
½ cucumber, sliced
80 g (2¾ oz/½ cup) peas, cooked al dente
½ red (Spanish) onion, thinly sliced
1 red capsicum (pepper), thinly sliced
2 tablespoons olive oil
juice of ½ lemon

TZATZIKI
½ cucumber
250 g (9 oz/1 cup) low fat natural yoghurt
1 garlic clove, crushed
juice of ½ lemon
1 tablespoon chopped mint

1 To make the tzatziki, grate the cucumber into a bowl. Wrap the cucumber flesh in a tea towel and squeeze out the water. Mix the cucumber with the remaining tzatziki ingredients.

2 Heat a non-stick frying pan or char-grill pan over medium heat and spray with a little olive oil. Season the lamb with pepper and cook for 3 minutes on each side—the meat should still be pink in the middle. Remove from the pan and allow to rest for a few minutes before slicing.

3 Meanwhile, mix together the rocket, spinach, tomatoes, cucumber, peas, onion and capsicum in a bowl.

4 Make a dressing by combining the oil and lemon juice in a screw-top jar, season with pepper and shake well. Drizzle the dressing over the salad, then divide the salad between four plates. Lay the lamb slices over the salad and top with a generous spoonful of tzatziki.

GI LOW G
Per serve
1280 kJ (305 Cal), 14 g fat (saturated 3 g),
33 g protein, 10 g carbohydrate, 4 g fibre,
155 mg sodium

WARM VEGETABLE SALAD SERVES 2

This salad makes it easy to boost your vegetable intake—something we are all being urged to do. The lemon yoghurt dressing is delicious with all sorts of vegetables, so try it with zucchini (courgettes), sweet potato or pumpkin, for a change.

Preparation time: 10 minutes Cooking time: 3 minutes

1 large carrot, sliced
4 florets cauliflower, broken into small pieces
4 florets broccoli, broken into small pieces
20 green beans, trimmed and halved
2 tablespoons chopped flat-leaf (Italian) parsley

LEMON YOGHURT DRESSING
2 tablespoons low fat natural yoghurt
2 tablespoons lemon juice
2 teaspoons pure floral honey
1 teaspoon crushed garlic
freshly ground black pepper

1 To blanch the vegetables, bring a saucepan of water to the boil. Add the carrot and cauliflower and cook for 2 minutes. Add the broccoli and beans and cook for a further 1 minute.

2 Meanwhile, make the lemon yoghurt dressing. Combine all the ingredients in a screw-top jar and shake to combine.

3 Drain the vegetables and refresh briefly under cold water. Pat dry, then place the vegetables in a bowl and pour over the dressing, tossing to coat. Sprinkle with parsley and serve.

ACTIVITY TIP
Be an active role model for your family—if you exercise, your partner and children are more likely to.

G GI LOW
Per serve
350 kJ (85 Cal), trace fat (saturated 0 g),
6 g protein, 13 g carbohydrate, 6 g fibre,
60 mg sodium

SWEET AND SOUR CHICKEN SALAD SERVES 2

Bulgur wheat is a versatile low GI cereal grain made from hard durum wheat that has been steamed, cracked and dried. It is also known as burghul and sometimes referred to as cracked wheat. You can buy 'ready-to-eat' versions from your supermarket. Use it in tabbouli or add to pilafs, vegetable burgers, stuffings, stews and even soups. Preparation time: 20 minutes Cooking time: 15 minutes

12 green beans, trimmed
8 thin asparagus spears, trimmed
12 snow peas (mangetout)
1 whole cooked skinless chicken breast fillet (about 240 g/8¹/² oz), sliced or shredded
60 g (2 oz/2 cups) baby rocket leaves

SWEET AND SOUR DRESSING
1 tablespoon white wine vinegar
1 tablespoon extra-virgin olive oil
2 teaspoons finely chopped preserved lemon
2 teaspoons raw (demerara) sugar
freshly ground black pepper

MINTED BULGUR WHEAT
90 g (3 oz/¹/² cup) bulgur wheat
125 ml (4 fl oz/¹/² cup) boiling water
2 tablespoons finely chopped mint

1 To blanch the vegetables, bring a saucepan of water to the boil. Put the beans, asparagus and snow peas in the pan and cook for 1 minute. Drain under cold running water to cool quickly. Put the chicken, rocket and blanched vegetables in a serving bowl.

2 To make the sweet and sour dressing, combine the dressing ingredients in a screw-top jar, season with pepper and shake well to mix. Pour over the salad and toss to coat in the dressing.

3 To make the minted bulgur wheat, put the bulgur wheat in a bowl and pour over the boiling water. Stir well, then cover and steam for 15 minutes, or until the water has absorbed. Fluff up the grains with a fork, then stir in the chopped mint. Serve with the chicken salad.

COOK'S TIP
If you prefer, buy a cooked chicken (without stuffing) to save time. Alternatively, gently poach a whole chicken breast in a covered saucepan in chicken stock (add a few leaves of fresh mint for extra flavour) for about 10 minutes, or until the chicken is tender and cooked through. Remove from the saucepan, wrap in foil and set aside until cool enough to slice.

GI LOW Ⓖ
Per serve
1968 kJ (469 Cal), 17 g fat (saturated 3 g),
35 g protein, 39 g carbohydrate, 9 g fibre,
110 mg sodium

ROAST PUMPKIN AND CHICKPEA SALAD SERVES 4–6

This sun-dried tomato dressing is not only delicious with pumpkin and chickpeas but can also be tossed through pasta, potatoes or steamed vegetables. Soaking time: Overnight Preparation time: 15 minutes Cooking time: 1¹⁄₂ hours

220 g (7³⁄₄ oz/1 cup) chickpeas,
soaked overnight in water
750 g (1 lb 10 oz) pumpkin,
cut into large cubes
olive oil spray
2 tablespoons chopped coriander
or mint leaves

SUN-DRIED TOMATO DRESSING
1¹⁄₂ tablespoons red wine vinegar
40 g (1¹⁄₂ oz/¹⁄₄ cup) sun-dried tomatoes
2 tablespoons extra-virgin olive oil
1 garlic clove
2 teaspoons balsamic vinegar
2 teaspoons sugar
2 teaspoons lemon juice
freshly ground black pepper

1 Drain the chickpeas from the soaking water and rinse. Put the chickpeas in a large saucepan and cover with fresh water. Bring to the boil and cook for 40–50 minutes, or until tender. Drain and allow to cool.

2 Preheat the oven to 200°C (400°F/Gas 6). Put the pumpkin on a baking tray lined with baking paper. Spray the pumpkin with olive oil and roast for 30–40 minutes, or until the pumpkin is tender and lightly caramelised. Allow to cool.

3 To make the sun-dried tomato dressing, put the red wine vinegar and tomatoes in a saucepan over low heat. Allow the tomatoes to soak in the hot vinegar to soften. Transfer the softened tomatoes to the bowl of a food processor and add the remaining dressing ingredients. Process to combine (don't overprocess—the texture should remain a little chunky).

4 Toss the pumpkin and chickpeas in the dressing, place in individual serving bowls or on a platter and sprinkle with the coriander or mint.

COOK'S TIPS

If you don't have a food processor, roughly chop the softened tomatoes by hand, as we have done here, then combine with the remaining dressing ingredients.

Dried chickpeas are used here, and need to be soaked overnight before cooking. To save time, substitute with canned chickpeas.

G GI LOW

Per serve (6)
1020 kJ (243 Cal), 10 g fat (saturated 2 g),
9 g protein, 24 g carbohydrate, 7 g fibre,
15 mg sodium

Recipe: Julie Le Clerc

GREEN PEA SOUP SERVES 4

Preparation time: 10 minutes Cooking time: 15 minutes

2 tablespoons olive oil
2 garlic cloves, crushed
1 onion, chopped
1 litre (35 fl oz/4 cups) chicken stock
500 g (1 lb 2 oz/3¼ cups) frozen green peas, defrosted
2 tablespoons chopped mint
2 tablespoons chopped parsley
freshly ground black pepper
2 lean rashers bacon, diced

1 Heat the oil in a frying pan over medium heat, add the garlic and onion and cook for 5 minutes, or until the onion is soft, taking care not to brown the onion. Add the stock, peas, mint and parsley. Bring to the boil, then reduce to a simmer for 8 minutes. Remove from the heat, allow to cool a little, then purée in a food processor or blender. Season with pepper.

2 Put the bacon under the grill and cook until crispy. Alternatively, dry-fry the bacon in a frying pan until crispy. Ladle the soup into four warmed bowls and garnish with the crispy bacon.

GI LOW Ⓖ

Per serve
900 kJ (214 Cal), 12 g fat (saturated 2 g),
12 g protein, 12 g carbohydrate, 8 g fibre,
1060 mg sodium

BARLEY AND VEGETABLE SOUP SERVES 4

Preparation time: 15 minutes Cooking time: 40 minutes

1 teaspoon olive oil
1 onion, chopped
100 g (3½ oz) carrots, diced
400 g (14 oz) can tomatoes
1 tablespoon tomato paste (purée)
110 g (3¾ oz/½ cup) pearl barley
1 litre (35 fl oz/4 cups) vegetable stock
100 g (3½ oz/⅔ cup) fresh or frozen peas
100 g (3½ oz) baby spinach leaves, shredded
15 g (½ oz/¼ cup) mixed herbs, such as parsley, basil and oregano, roughly chopped
freshly ground black pepper

1 Heat the oil in a heavy-based frying pan, add the onion and cook, covered, over low heat for about 5 minutes, or until the onion is soft. Add the carrots, tomatoes, tomato paste, barley and stock. Bring to the boil, then reduce the heat and simmer for 30 minutes. Add the peas and simmer for 2–3 minutes, then add the spinach and herbs and simmer for a further 1–2 minutes.

2 Divide the hot soup between four bowls. Season with pepper and serve with low GI bread of your choice, if desired.

GI LOW Ⓖ

Per serve
720 kJ (170 Cal), 3 g fat (saturated <1 g),
6 g protein, 27 g carbohydrate, 8 g fibre,
890 mg sodium

Recipe: Penny Hunking, Energise Nutrition

LENTIL, SPINACH AND FETA SALAD SERVES 4

The slightly peppery tasting Puy lentils are ideal for salads because they hold their shape when cooked, although they tend to take a little longer to cook than other lentils. Use brown lentils as a substitute if Puy are not available, but watch the cooking times as they can turn mushy if you overcook them. Preparation time: 10 minutes Cooking time: 35 minutes

200 g (7 oz/1 cup) Puy lentils
2 garlic cloves, flattened with the side of a knife
2 red capsicums (peppers)
150 g (5¼ oz) baby spinach leaves
90 g (3 oz) reduced fat feta cheese, cubed
1 tablespoon good-quality olive oil
2 teaspoons balsamic vinegar
1 teaspoon sugar

1 Put the lentils in a saucepan, cover with water, add the flattened garlic cloves and bring to the boil. Reduce the heat and simmer for 25 minutes, or until the lentils are soft (these lentils should retain their shape). Remove the garlic and drain.

2 Quarter the capsicums and remove the seeds. Place the capsicum pieces, skin-side up, under a grill and cook until the skins are completely black. Allow to cool for 6–8 minutes, then remove the skins. Slice the flesh into strips.

3 Combine the lentils, capsicum, spinach and feta cheese in a serving bowl. Pour over the oil and balsamic vinegar, sprinkle with sugar and mix well. Serve at room temperature.

ACTIVITY TIP
Arrange social get-togethers that involve some activity rather than centered solely on eating and drinking—meet for a walk, go bowling or have a picnic in the park.

G GI LOW
Per serve
1115 kJ (265 Cal), 9 g fat (saturated 3 g),
20 g protein, 23 g carbohydrate, 9 g fibre,
260 mg sodium

GOLDEN CARROT SOUP SERVES 4

Soups are wonderfully filling, full of nutrients and if you make them right provide all this with few kilojoules—great for any weight loss program. Use winter carrots for this soup, as they have more flavour than the tiny spring and summer carrots.

Preparation time: 10 minutes Cooking time: 25 minutes

2 tablespoons olive oil
5 large winter carrots (about 1 kg/
2 lb 4 oz), diced
1 large onion, chopped
2 garlic cloves, crushed
3 bay leaves
1.25 litres (44 fl oz/5 cups) beef or
chicken stock
freshly ground black pepper
flat-leaf (Italian) parsley, to serve

1 Heat the oil in a large saucepan. Add the carrots, onion, garlic and bay leaves and cook for 10 minutes.

2 Put the stock in another saucepan and bring to the boil. Pour the boiling stock over the vegetables and simmer for 15 minutes, or until tender. Remove the pan from the heat and remove the bay leaves. Allow the soup to cool a little, then transfer to a food processor or blender and purée until smooth. Season with pepper. If the soup is too thick, add some extra stock. Serve garnished with parsley.

COOK'S TIP
As a variation, garnish the soup with small pieces of grilled bacon, or top with a dollop of garlic-flavoured low fat yoghurt.

GI LOW Ⓖ
Per serve
745 kJ (180 Cal), 10 g fat (saturated 2 g),
5 g protein, 17 g carbohydrate, 8 g fibre,
850 mg sodium

Recipe: Steffan Rössner

SMOKED SALMON AND DILL WITH PASTA SALAD SERVES 4–6

This special-occasion salad makes a light meal for four or an exquisite starter for six. If serving as a main meal, accompany with a cucumber salad tossed with an oil and vinegar dressing. Preparation time: 15 minutes Cooking time: 10 minutes

250 g (9 oz) penne rigate pasta
150 g (5¼ oz) smoked salmon, cut into strips
6 cherry tomatoes, halved,
or quartered if large
6 spring onions, thinly sliced on the diagonal
1 small red (Spanish) onion, cut into
thin rings, slices separated
200 g (7 oz) low fat natural yoghurt (optional)

DRESSING
80 ml (2½ fl oz/⅓ cup) extra-virgin olive oil
3 spring onions, chopped
juice of ½ lemon
30 g (1 oz/½ cup) chopped dill
freshly ground black pepper

1 To make the dressing, combine the oil, spring onions, lemon juice and dill in a food processor and purée until smooth. Season with pepper.

2 Cook the penne in plenty of boiling water until al dente. Drain and rinse under cold running water until cool. Drain well and place in the serving dish. Pour over the dressing, then add the smoked salmon, tomatoes, spring onions and onion rings. Toss gently to coat the pasta in the dressing. Serve with a dollop of yoghurt, if using.

COOK'S TIPS

Penne rigate is a finely ridged penne. Ridged or ribbed pastas tend to hold on to more sauce than smooth pastas.

Avoid overcooking your pasta—not only does al dente pasta taste better, but it has a lower GI than pasta that has been cooked for too long.

G GI LOW
Per serve (6)
1330 kJ (315 Cal), 14 g fat (saturated 2 g),
13 g protein, 33 g carbohydrate, 3 g fibre,
460 mg sodium

Recipe: Loukie Werle, Trattoria Pasta

BARBECUED CHILLI MINT LAMB AND TOMATO SALAD SERVES 2

This tasty salad uses the classic flavour combination of lamb, mint and tomatoes. Serve the zesty bulgur on the side, or toss it through the salad at the end, as we've done here. Preparation time: 20 minutes Cooking time: 25 minutes

250 g (9 oz) lamb fillet, trimmed
extra-virgin olive oil, for brushing
30 g (1 oz/1 cup) mint leaves, roughly torn
4 small vine-ripened tomatoes, cut into
eighths, or 8 cherry tomatoes, halved
½ red capsicum (pepper), sliced into strips
1 Lebanese (short) cucumber, sliced
into rounds
1 red chilli, seeds removed and
thinly sliced (optional)
freshly ground black pepper
2 teaspoons extra-virgin olive oil
juice of ½ lemon

ZESTY BULGUR WHEAT
90 g (3 oz/½ cup) bulgur wheat
125 ml (4 fl oz/½ cup) boiling water
finely grated zest and juice of 1 lemon

1 Lightly brush the lamb fillet with a little oil. Cook on a preheated barbecue or in a char-grill pan for 3–4 minutes each side, or until cooked to your liking. Remove the meat, wrap in foil and leave it to rest for 10 minutes.

2 Put the mint, tomatoes, capsicum, cucumber and chilli, if using, in a serving bowl. Season with pepper. Make a dressing by combining the oil and lemon juice in a screw-top jar and shake well.

3 To make the zesty bulgur wheat, put the bulgur wheat in a bowl and pour over the boiling water. Cover with foil (or plastic wrap or a plate) and leave to steam for about 15 minutes, or until the water has absorbed. Fluff up the grains with a fork and stir in the lemon zest and juice.

4 Slice the lamb fillet thinly across the grain, toss with the salad ingredients and the bulgur wheat, then pour over the dressing and toss to coat.

ACTIVITY TIP
A recent study found that those who walked regularly with a dog lost more weight than those who walked alone. If you don't have your own dog, offer to walk a neighbour's—you will both end up reaping the rewards.

GI LOW Ⓖ
Per serve
1702 kJ (405 Cal), 11 g fat (saturated 3 g),
34 g protein, 37 g carbohydrate, 10 g fibre,
117 mg sodium

COUSCOUS SALAD SERVES 4–6

Although couscous has a medium GI, combining it with chickpeas, as we have done here, means that the overall meal has a low GI. This couscous salad is delicious as a meal in itself or serve as an accompaniment for chicken or meat dishes.
Preparation time: 15 minutes

185 g (6½ oz/1 cup) couscous
170 g (6 oz/1 cup) canned chickpeas, rinsed and drained
50 g (1¾ oz/½ small bunch) flat-leaf (Italian) parsley, chopped
40 g (1½ oz/½ small bunch) coriander, leaves picked and chopped
1 tablespoon ground cumin
½ red capsicum (pepper), chopped
½ green capsicum (pepper), chopped
180 g (6¼ oz/1 cup) chopped mixed dried fruit, such as apricots, dates, currants, figs
2 tablespoons pistachio nuts
2 tablespoons pine nuts, toasted

DRESSING
2 tablespoons extra-virgin olive oil
juice of 1 lemon
freshly ground black pepper

1 Make the couscous according to the packet instructions—you should end up with about 450 g (1 lb/2 cups) cooked couscous. Make sure the couscous is quite dry before using it.

2 Put the couscous in a large serving bowl and combine with the chickpeas, herbs, cumin, capsicums, dried fruit, pistachios and pine nuts.

3 To make the dressing, put the oil and lemon juice in a screw-top jar. Season with pepper, shake well, then pour over the couscous salad and toss to coat.

ⓖ GI LOW
Per serve (6)
1029 kJ (245 Cal), 13 g fat (saturated 1 g),
6 g protein, 25 g carbohydrate, 5 g fibre,
12 mg sodium

CHICKEN, MINT AND CORN SOUP SERVES 4

For the sweetest flavour, buy corn on the cob with the husk intact, because the natural sugar in the kernels starts converting into starch the moment the green husk is removed. Fresh cooked corn has a low GI of 48. Frozen kernels are a suitable substitute for fresh in this recipe. Preparation time: 10 minutes Cooking time: 20 minutes

2 corn cobs
1 litre (35 fl oz/4 cups) good-quality
chicken stock
6 mint leaves, plus extra to garnish
4 x 160 g (5½ oz) skinless chicken
breast fillets
60 g (2 oz) snow pea sprouts
2 teaspoons julienned preserved lemon rind
¼ teaspoon salt
freshly ground black pepper

1 Put the corn cobs in a large saucepan of boiling water and cook for 10 minutes. Remove the cobs and cut off the kernels. Set aside.

2 Put the chicken stock and mint leaves in a poaching pan or large saucepan and bring to the boil. Add the chicken, return to a simmer and poach for 10–12 minutes, or until the chicken is cooked through. Just before the chicken is ready, add the corn kernels and snow pea sprouts to the hot stock.

3 Remove the chicken, slice on the diagonal, then divide between four bowls. Ladle the broth and vegetables into the bowls. Garnish with the preserved lemon and extra mint and season with salt and pepper.

GI LOW Ⓖ

Per serve
1315 kJ (315 Cal), 10 g fat (saturated 3 g),
39 g protein, 16 g carbohydrate, 4 g fibre,
984 mg sodium

Recipe: Luke Mangan

CURRIED LENTIL SALAD SERVES 4

One of our key guidelines in The Low GI Diet *is to eat more legumes such as beans, chickpeas and lentils—in fact, we recommend you have a meal that includes legumes at least twice a week. This curried lentil salad will make that easy!*

Preparation time: 10 minutes   Cooking time: 20–25 minutes

1 tablespoon unsaturated margarine
1 tablespoon curry powder
300 g (10½ oz/1½ cups) Puy lentils
1 small red (Spanish) onion, thinly sliced
125 g (4½ oz/¾ cup) cherry tomatoes, halved
60 g (2 oz) baby spinach leaves
7 g (¼ oz/¼ cup) coriander leaves
5 g (⅛ oz/¼ cup) mint leaves
2 tablespoons red wine vinegar
2 tablespoons extra-virgin olive oil
sea salt and freshly ground black pepper

1 Melt the margarine in a saucepan and add the curry powder. Stir for about 20 seconds, then add the lentils, stirring to coat well. Add a generous pinch of salt. Cover the lentils with water, bring to a simmer and cook for about 20 minutes, or until the lentils are soft. (Take care not to let the lentils boil dry—top up with more water if necessary, but don't make them too wet.) Remove from the heat, drain, rinse and set aside to cool.

2 Put the cooled lentils in a large bowl with the onion, tomatoes, spinach and herbs. Whisk together the vinegar and oil, pour over the salad and toss well. Season to taste with sea salt and pepper.

G GI LOW
Per serve
1395 kJ (332 Cal), 14 g fat (saturated 2 g),
18 g protein, 29 g carbohydrate, 12 g fibre,
356 mg sodium

Luke Mangan is one of Australia's best-known and talented chefs. He has opened three restaurants in Sydney: Salt (which won two chef's hats), Bistro Lulu, and Moorish. In 2004 he was invited to cook for the wedding festivities of Crown Prince Frederik and Mary Donaldson in Denmark and he has also cooked for other guests such as Bill Clinton and Sir Richard Branson. Sir Richard Branson consequently appointed him food consultant for Virgin Atlantic Airways on the Sydney-to-London route launched in December 2004. Author of three cookbooks—*Breakfast, Lunch, Dinner (BLD)*; *Luke Mangan Food*; and *Luke Mangan Classics*—Luke is also the food presenter on Channel Nine's The Today Show. He also travels widely, promoting Australian food and wine.

SOBA NOODLE SOUP WITH PRAWNS AND TOFU SERVES 4

Tofu, whether you buy the soft or firm variety, absorbs other flavours well and makes a delicious addition to stir-fries and soups such as this one. Preparation time: 20 minutes Cooking time: 10 minutes

100 g (3½ oz) soba noodles
1 litre (35 fl oz/4 cups) vegetable stock
2 teaspoons grated ginger
2 tablespoons soy sauce
1 tablespoon mirin
2 teaspoons caster sugar
1–2 small red chillies, seeded and finely chopped
24 raw prawns, peeled and deveined, with tails intact
2 spring onions, sliced on the diagonal
50 g (1¾ oz) baby spinach leaves, shredded
300 g (10½ oz) silken firm tofu, cut into 2 cm (¾ in) cubes
7 g (¼ oz/¼ cup) coriander leaves

1 Cook the soba noodles in a saucepan of boiling water for 4 minutes, or until tender. Drain and set aside.

2 Combine the stock, ginger, soy sauce, mirin, sugar and chillies in a large saucepan. Bring to the boil, then reduce the heat and simmer for 3 minutes. Add the prawns, spring onions and spinach and simmer for 2 minutes, or until the prawns turn pink and are cooked.

3 Divide the noodles and tofu evenly between four bowls. Spoon over the broth and serve garnished with coriander.

COOK'S TIP
The sodium content of this recipe can be reduced by using either a home-made or a low salt vegetable stock, and a salt-reduced soy sauce.

GI LOW ⓖ
Per serve
1225 kJ (290 Cal), 6 g fat (saturated 1 g),
38 g protein, 23 g carbohydrate, 2 g fibre,
1160 mg sodium

FRAGRANT BULGUR WHEAT WITH ZEST SERVES 4

Bulgur wheat is used extensively in Middle Eastern cooking and not only has a low GI (48) but is delicious and takes only minutes to prepare. Try this salad as an accompaniment to chicken, or pan-fried marinated tofu slices for a vegetarian meal.
Preparation time: 15 minutes Cooking time: 17 minutes

175 g (6 oz/1 cup) bulgur wheat
250 ml (9 fl oz/1 cup) boiling water
1 tablespoon olive oil
1 tablespoon finely chopped lemon grass
1 tablespoon grated ginger
grated zest of ½ lemon
grated zest of ½ lime
1 tablespoon lemon juice
1 tablespoon lime juice
2 vine-ripened tomatoes, chopped
4 spring onions, thinly sliced on the diagonal
175 g (6 oz/1 bunch) asparagus, blanched, cut on the diagonal into 2.5 cm (1 in) pieces
freshly ground black pepper
2 tablespoons chopped parsley

LEMON YOGHURT
250 g (9 oz/1 cup) low fat natural yoghurt
1 tablespoon lemon juice
2 tablespoons chopped chives

1 Put the bulgur wheat in a bowl and pour over the boiling water. Stir well, then cover with foil (or plastic wrap or a plate) and steam for 15 minutes, or until the water has absorbed.

2 Heat the oil in a non-stick frying pan over medium heat, add the lemon grass and ginger and fry for 2 minutes. Add the lemon and lime zest and juice. Add the bulgur wheat and mix well. Transfer to a serving bowl and add the tomatoes, spring onions and asparagus and toss to combine. Season with pepper and sprinkle with parsley.

3 To make the lemon yoghurt, put all the ingredients in a bowl and mix to combine, adding a little more lemon juice if it is too thick. To serve, drizzle the yoghurt over the bulgur wheat salad.

Ⓖ GI LOW
Per serve
1160 kJ (275 Cal), 6 g fat (saturated 1 g),
12 g protein, 38 g carbohydrate, 8 g fibre,
70 mg sodium

Recipe: Jill McMillan

BLACK BEAN SOUP SERVES 4–6

This tangy, nourishing soup shows you how easy it is to incorporate legumes into your weekly meal plans. Black beans, also called turtle beans, have a mild, earthy taste when cooked. They are widely used throughout Latin America and the Caribbean.

Soaking time: Overnight Preparation time: 15 minutes Cooking time: 1 hour

200 g (7 oz/1 cup) dried black beans, soaked overnight in water
1 tablespoon olive oil
2 onions, roughly chopped
2 garlic cloves, crushed
3 rashers bacon, fat trimmed, diced
2 teaspoons ground cumin
1 teaspoon ground coriander
2 carrots, diced
450 g (1 lb) orange sweet potato, diced
2 bay leaves
1.5 litres (52 fl oz/6 cups) chicken or vegetable stock
15 g (½ oz/¼ cup) chopped coriander leaves
freshly ground black pepper

1 Drain the black beans from the soaking water, then rinse under cold water and drain again.

2 Heat the oil in a large saucepan. Add the onions, garlic and bacon and cook for 4 minutes, or until the onion is soft. Add the cumin and ground coriander and cook for about 30 seconds, or until aromatic. Add the carrots, sweet potato, bay leaves, stock and beans. Bring to the boil, then cover and simmer over low heat for 1 hour, or until the beans and vegetables are soft.

3 Remove the bay leaves from the soup. Allow to cool a little, then transfer to a food processor or blender and purée until smooth. Stir in the coriander and season with pepper.

COOK'S TIPS

Although they will keep indefinitely, it's best to use legumes within 1 year of purchase. Before cooking, be sure to pick through them, picking out any small pebbles, split and withered beans and any other foreign matter.

Don't add salt to the cooking water—it slows down water absorption and cooking takes longer.

You can keep soaked or cooked beans in an airtight container for several days in the refrigerator.

GI LOW Ⓖ
Per serve (6)
960 kJ (230 Cal), 4 g fat (saturated <1 g),
13 g protein, 35 g carbohydrate, 8 g fibre,
390 mg sodium

BORLOTTI BEAN SALAD SERVES 4

Preparation time: 10 minutes Cooking time: 2 minutes

175 g (6 oz/1 bunch) asparagus, trimmed
2 teaspoons pure floral honey
2 teaspoons olive oil
2 tablespoons red wine vinegar
250 g (9 oz/1½ cups) cherry tomatoes, halved
400 g (14 oz) can borlotti beans, rinsed and drained
2 tablespoons chopped parsley
freshly ground black pepper

1 Bring a large frying pan filled with water to a gentle simmer. Place the asparagus in the water and cook for 1–2 minutes, or until tender. Refresh under cold water, then chop into 3 cm (1¼ in) lengths.

2 To make a dressing for the bean salad, put the honey, oil and vinegar in a small screw-top jar and shake to combine.

3 Put the tomatoes, beans, parsley and cooled asparagus in a bowl. Pour over the dressing, toss to combine, then season with pepper.

Ⓖ GI LOW

Per serve
550 kJ (130 Cal), 3 g fat (trace saturated),
7 g protein, 21 g carbohydrate, 4 g fibre,
7 mg sodium

SWEET CHILLI TUNA SALAD SERVES 2

Preparation time: 10 minutes

4 iceberg lettuce leaves, shredded
6 cm (2½ in) wide strip of red capsicum (pepper), finely diced
1 tomato, diced
½ red (Spanish) onion, finely chopped
2 x 95 g (3¼ oz) cans sweet chilli tuna
35 g (1¼ oz/1 cup) crispy soy noodles
juice of 1 lime
coriander leaves, to garnish

1 Combine the lettuce, capsicum, tomato and onion in a serving bowl. Add the tuna and noodles. Squeeze the lime juice over, add the coriander leaves and toss to combine. Serve immediately.

COOK'S TIP
If you can't find canned sweet chilli tuna, use canned tuna in springwater and add 1 tablespoon sweet chilli sauce to each can.

Ⓖ GI LOW

Per serve
1215 kJ (290 Cal), 10 g fat (saturated 3 g),
28 g protein, 20 g carbohydrate, 7 g fibre,
560 mg sodium

Right: Sweet chilli tuna salad

VIETNAMESE BEEF SOUP SERVES 4

Pho bo, a beef soup with rice noodles, is often referred to as Vietnam's national dish and is eaten at any time of day. A boiling broth is poured over the thinly sliced raw beef and is hot enough to cook the beef. Separate aromatic seasonings such as chillies and Vietnamese mint are often served on the side. Preparation time: 20 minutes Cooking time: 35 minutes

500 g (1 lb 2 oz) fresh rice noodles
200 g (7 oz) beef eye fillet, very thinly sliced
100 g (3½ oz) bean sprouts
2 tablespoons roughly chopped coriander leaves
4 spring onions, thinly sliced
1–2 small red chillies, to taste, seeded and very thinly sliced
½ lime, cut into wedges

STOCK
2 teaspoons olive oil
1 garlic clove, finely chopped
1 small brown onion, chopped
4 cm (1½ in) piece ginger, thinly sliced
1.5 litres (52 fl oz/6 cups) beef stock
1 cinnamon stick
1 star anise
1 lemon grass stick, lightly bruised
1 tablespoon fish sauce
1 tablespoon soy sauce
1 teaspoon caster sugar

1 To make the stock, heat the oil in a large saucepan and add the garlic, onion and ginger and stir-fry until aromatic. Add 1 litre (35 fl oz/4 cups) water, stock, cinnamon, star anise, lemon grass, fish sauce, soy sauce and sugar. Bring to the boil, then reduce the heat and simmer, uncovered, for 30 minutes. Strain the stock, return the liquid to the pan and return to a boil.

2 Put the fresh rice noodles in a bowl, cover with boiling water and leave to soak for a few minutes. When the noodles have softened a little, gently separate them, then drain. Divide the noodles between four deep bowls, top with the beef slices, bean sprouts and coriander, then pour over the boiling stock. Garnish with spring onions and chillies and serve with the lime wedges for squeezing over.

ACTIVITY TIP

For all short journeys that would take less than 5 minutes in the car, take the time to walk instead. Go shopping on foot and carry your bags home—a fantastic total body workout! However, if you have to drive to the nearest shopping centre, park the car in the furthest parking spot and walk the rest of the way.

GI LOW G
Per serve
960 kJ (230 Cal), 5 g fat (saturated 1 g),
15 g protein, 30 g carbohydrate, 2 g fibre,
830 mg sodium

Recipe: Lynne Mullins, Noodles to Pasta

DINNER

WHAT'S FOR DINNER? HERE'S HOW WE DO IT.
WE CHOOSE THE CARBOHYDRATE: SWEET
POTATO, RICE, PASTA, NOODLES, GRAINS,
LEGUMES OR A COMBINATION. THEN WE ADD
VEGETABLES—LOTS OF THEM—EITHER FRESH,
FROZEN OR CANNED. FINALLY, WE INCLUDE
PROTEIN FOR NUTRIENTS, FLAVOUR AND FILL-UP
VALUE, BUT WE MAKE SURE IT'S LOW
IN SATURATED FAT.

TUNA POACHED IN TOMATO AND FENNEL WITH CHILLI CHICKPEA MASH SERVES 4

Mashed legumes make a great low GI and nutrient-rich alternative to mashed potatoes. The mash also makes a delicious spread on its own, rather like hommous—if you like it hot, add extra chilli. Preparation time: 20 minutes Cooking time: 45 minutes

1 tablespoon extra-virgin olive oil
2 large fennel bulbs or 4 baby fennel bulbs, thickly sliced (tops reserved)
1 large red (Spanish) onion, sliced
2 garlic cloves, finely chopped
440 g (15½ oz) can peeled chopped tomatoes, or tomato pieces
250 ml (9 fl oz/1 cup) dry white wine
5 cm (2 in) long strip of lemon zest
1 bay leaf
500 g (1 lb 2 oz) tuna steaks, cut into large bite-sized chunks
freshly ground black pepper
2 tablespoons chopped flat-leaf (Italian) parsley
1 tablespoon chopped fennel tops
lemon wedges, to serve

CHILLI CHICKPEA MASH
440 g (15½ oz) can chickpeas, rinsed and drained
1 small red chilli, seeded and thinly sliced
2 tablespoons chopped flat-leaf (Italian) parsley
juice of ½ lemon
125 ml (4 fl oz/½ cup) boiling water
freshly ground black pepper

1 Heat the oil in a flameproof casserole dish over low heat and gently cook the sliced fennel, onion and garlic for 10 minutes, or until the onion is golden and transparent. Add the tomatoes, wine, lemon zest and bay leaf and stir to combine all the ingredients. Bring to a simmer and cook, covered, for about 30 minutes, or until the vegetables are just cooked.

2 Place the tuna chunks in the vegetable mixture, gently stir, then poach for 3–4 minutes.

3 While the tuna is poaching, make the chilli chickpea mash. Put the chickpeas in a food processor with the chilli, parsley and lemon juice and purée, adding just enough of the boiling water to make a smooth, creamy mixture. Season with pepper.

4 Remove the strip of lemon zest and bay leaf from the tuna and season with pepper. Place a scoop of warm chilli chickpea mash onto each plate and top with the tuna and vegetable mixture. Scatter over the chopped parsley and fennel tops. Serve with lemon wedges, and with crunchy grainy bread for mopping up the juices, if desired.

COOK'S TIP
Fennel is delicious thinly sliced and served raw in salads or cooked. Choose bulbs with green, sweet-smelling leaves. Remove the tough outer stalks as they are usually damaged or stringy, trim the base of the bulb, then halve, quarter, slice or dice. Chop the feathery tops and use as a garnish, or add to sauces or dressings at the end of cooking time.

Ⓖ GI LOW
Per serve
1730 kJ (410 Cal), 14 g fat (saturated 4 g),
39 g protein, 20 g carbohydrate, 9 g fibre,
360 mg sodium

VEAL TAGINE WITH SWEET POTATOES SERVES 4

The word tagine refers both to the Moroccan cooking pot—traditionally a round clay pot with a conical lid—as well as the stew you cook in it. If you don't have a tagine, a flameproof casserole dish will do just as well. For the best results, make your own tagine spice mix; otherwise, buy a ready-made mix. Preparation time: 20 minutes Cooking time: 1¼ hours

500 g (1 lb 2 oz) veal, trimmed and cut into 2.5 cm (1 in) cubes
2 tablespoons extra-virgin olive oil
2 red (Spanish) onions, sliced
2 garlic cloves, crushed
4 tomatoes (about 300 g/10½ oz in total), quartered
2 orange sweet potatoes (about 500 g/ 1 lb 2 oz in total), thickly sliced
1 red capsicum (pepper), halved and sliced
15 g (½ oz/¼ cup) chopped coriander leaves (optional)

TAGINE SPICE MIX
5 teaspoons mild paprika
2 teaspoons ground coriander
1 teaspoon ground cassia bark or cinnamon
1 teaspoon cayenne pepper
½ teaspoon allspice
¼ teaspoon ground cloves
¼ teaspoon ground green cardamom

1 To make the tagine spice mix, combine all the spices in a large bowl.

2 To make the tagine, toss the veal in the spice mix to coat. Heat the oil in a flameproof casserole dish over high heat and quickly brown the meat pieces on all sides. Remove with a slotted spoon and set aside. Reduce the heat to medium, add the onions and garlic and cook gently for 5 minutes, or until the onions are golden and translucent.

3 Return the veal to the dish and add the tomatoes, sweet potatoes, capsicum and 250 ml (9 fl oz/1 cup) water. Stir gently to combine, then cover with a piece of baking paper (this helps reduce evaporation) and the lid and simmer gently for 1 hour, or until the meat is tender. Garnish with coriander, if using.

4 This tagine is a meal in itself, or you can serve with steamed basmati rice or bulgur wheat, if desired.

COOK'S TIP
The pods of green cardamom are bright green and not to be confused with brown cardamom, as they are not interchangeable in recipes. Green cardamom has a sweet eucalyptus-like aroma that adds 'fresh' notes to spice mixes. Brown has a distinct 'musty-smoky' flavour. You can buy green cardamom in larger supermarkets and specialist spice stores.

GI LOW Ⓖ
Per serve
1410 kJ (335 Cal), 12 g fat (saturated 2 g),
31 g protein, 23 g carbohydrate, 4 g fibre,
130 mg sodium

Tagine spice mix: Liz and Ian Hemphill, Herbies Spices

LINGUINE WITH SALMON AND PEAS SERVES 4

If you are a fan of the 'meal in a bowl', then this recipe is just right for you. It's also packed with sustaining low GI carbs, vegetables and protein for that perfect 'fill-up' factor. Best of all, it's on the table in around 30 minutes.

Preparation time: 15 minutes Cooking time: 17 minutes

350 g (12 oz) linguine
2 x 200 g (7 oz) salmon fillets, skinned
1 tablespoon extra-virgin olive oil
300 g (10½ oz/2 cups) fresh or frozen peas
250 ml (9 fl oz/1 cup) fish or vegetable stock
2 tablespoons chopped flat-leaf (Italian) parsley
freshly ground black pepper
juice of 1 lemon, or to taste
1 teaspoon finely grated lemon zest, or to taste

1 Bring a large saucepan of water to the boil and cook the pasta until al dente.

2 Meanwhile, check the salmon for any bones, then cut into bite-sized pieces. Heat the oil in a large, deep frying pan until the oil is shimmering, then add the salmon and cook gently for about 5 minutes, or until the salmon changes colour and is cooked through, being careful not to brown it. Add the peas, stock and parsley and cook for 1–2 minutes. Season with plenty of pepper, then add the lemon juice and zest, to taste, stirring gently to combine all the ingredients.

3 When the pasta is cooked, drain well and add to the sauce, tossing lightly to coat in the sauce. Serve immediately.

Ⓖ GI LOW

Per serve
2185 kJ (520 Cal), 13 g fat (saturated 2 g),
34 g protein, 66 g carbohydrate, 8 g fibre,
240 mg sodium

BEEF STROGANOFF SERVES 4

Beef stroganoff is usually fairly loaded with sour cream, which pushes up the saturated fat content. This version uses natural yoghurt instead of sour cream. The GI of this recipe is medium, which is due to the basmati rice—to lower the GI, you may prefer to use half rice and half barley. Preparation time: 15 minutes Cooking time: 20 minutes

300 g (10½ oz/1½ cups) basmati rice
500 g (1 lb 2 oz) lean beef, cut into strips
1 tablespoon olive oil
1 red (Spanish) onion, thinly sliced
1 brown onion, thinly sliced
2 large garlic cloves, crushed
250 g (9 oz) mushrooms, sliced
60 ml (2 fl oz/¼ cup) brandy (optional)
zest and juice of 1 orange
½ teaspoon dried dill or 1 tablespoon chopped dill
freshly ground black pepper
250 g (9 oz/1 cup) low fat natural yoghurt

1 Wash the rice and put it in a large saucepan with 500 ml (17 fl oz/2 cups) water. Cover with the lid and bring to the boil, then reduce the heat and simmer for 10 minutes. Turn off the heat and leave to stand, without removing the lid, until ready to serve.

2 Meanwhile, heat a large non-stick frying pan over medium heat. Dry-fry the meat, in small batches, for 2 minutes. Remove the meat and set aside.

3 Using the same pan, heat the oil over medium heat, add the onions and garlic and fry for 5 minutes, or until the onions are soft. Add the mushrooms and fry for 3 minutes. Return the meat to the pan.

4 If using brandy, pour it into the pan and flambé, then dowse the flames with the orange zest and orange juice. Add the dill and season with lots of pepper. Turn off the heat before mixing in the yoghurt.

5 Spoon the steamed rice onto plates and top with the stroganoff. You may like to serve this with a mixed green salad or steamed vegetables.

ACTIVITY TIP

Try out a new activity. For example, join a dance class: salsa, ballroom, line dancing, Scottish dancing or jazz; go rollerblading with friends; book in for golf or tennis lessons; or take your children to the park. You can't afford not to exercise, so find something you enjoy and get moving!

GI MEDIUM G

Per serve
2260 kJ (540 Cal), 10 g fat (saturated 3 g),
39 g protein, 70 g carbohydrate, 3 g fibre,
435 mg sodium

Recipe: Isobel McMillan

BAVETTE WITH FRESH MUSSELS SERVES 4–6

You can prepare the mussels and the sauce for this light, summery pasta dish in advance, and refrigerate if it's going to be longer than 1 hour before you cook the pasta, or leave at room temperature if you are planning to serve immediately.
Preparation time: 15 minutes Cooking time: 15 minutes

1 kg (2 lb 4 oz) fresh mussels
1 leek
80 ml (2½ fl oz/⅓ cup) extra-virgin olive oil
4 large garlic cloves, crushed with a knife blade
4 tablespoons chopped kalamata olives
4 tablespoons roughly torn basil leaves
juice of 1 lemon
freshly ground black pepper
350 g (12 oz) bavette pasta
lemon wedges, to serve

1 Clean the mussels by thoroughly scrubbing the shells with a brush. Pull out the hairy beards and discard any broken mussels or any open mussels that don't close when tapped on the bench. Rinse well.

2 Place the cleaned mussels in a large saucepan, with only the water clinging to them, and place the pan over high heat. Cover the pan and shake over the heat until all the mussels have opened. Discard any mussels that do not open. Remove the mussels from their shells and place in a large serving dish (leave a few mussels in their shells for garnish, if desired).

3 To make the sauce, clean the leek in several changes of cold water. When no grit remains, cut into julienne strips. Heat 1 tablespoon of the oil in a frying pan over medium heat, add the leek and cook for about 3 minutes, or until tender and slightly brown around the edges. Add to the mussels in the dish, along with the remaining oil, garlic cloves, olives, basil and lemon juice. Season with pepper.

4 Cook the bavette in plenty of boiling salted water until al dente. Remove the crushed garlic cloves from the mussel mixture. Drain the pasta, add to the mussels and toss well. Serve immediately with lemon wedges.

COOK'S TIP
Bavette pasta is a long flat-ribbon pasta similar to tagliatelle but narrower. If unavailable, use tagliatelle or spaghetti.

GI LOW
Per serve (6)
1950 kJ (465 Cal), 16 g fat (saturated 3 g),
27 g protein, 52 g carbohydrate, 3 g fibre,
1127 mg sodium

Recipe: Loukie Werle, Trattoria Pasta

PASTA WITH CAULIFLOWER AND PANCETTA SERVES 4

We love this recipe from Antonio Carluccio, which is based on the old traditions of combining pasta with vegetables. Its simplicity and gutsy flavours are just right. Preparation time: 5 minutes Cooking time: 20 minutes

600 g (1 lb 5 oz) cauliflower florets
400 g (14 oz) dried cavatelli or penne pasta
1 tablespoon olive oil
125 g (4½ oz) pancetta, finely diced
1 small red chilli, finely chopped
50 g (1¾ oz) aged pecorino cheese, grated
2 tablespoons roughly chopped parsley
1 teaspoon salt

1 Cook the cauliflower and pasta together in plenty of boiling, salted water for 18 minutes, or until the cauliflower is cooked and the pasta is al dente.

2 Meanwhile, heat the oil in a frying pan, add the pancetta and chilli and fry for 3 minutes, or until starting to brown.

3 Drain the pasta and cauliflower and place on a large serving plate or in individual bowls. Sprinkle with the cheese, then tip the pancetta and chilli over the top. Add the parsley and season with salt. Mix well in the bowl before serving.

COOK'S TIP
The original version of this recipe, published in *Antonio Carluccio's Vegetables*, uses 2 tablespoons olive oil, 250 g (9 oz) pancetta and 100 g (3½ oz) aged pecorino cheese. Our version is a little lower in fat.

In 1999, Antonio Carluccio received Italy's highest honour, the *Commendatore Omri*, in recognition of his services to his native country. He is the proprietor of London's Neal Street Restaurant and, together with his wife Priscilla, created the specialist Italian food shop Carluccio's and a series of Carluccio's Caffés. A renowned authority on the subject of wild food in particular and Italian cooking in general, he has presented two hugely popular television series—Antonio Carluccio's Northern Italian Feast and Southern Italian Feast—and has made many appearances on BBC2's Food and Drink. He has also written several bestselling books, including *Antonio Carluccio's Passion for Pasta*, *Carluccio's Complete Italian Food* and *Antonio Carluccio Goes Wild*.

GI LOW Ⓖ
Per serve
2130 kJ (510 Cal), 14 g fat (saturated 5 g),
24 g protein, 71 g carbohydrate, 6 g fibre,
1180 mg sodium

SPINACH AND RICOTTA CANNELLONI SERVES 4

This delicious dinner dish is easy to assemble using today's wonderful convenience foods. Buy a really good-quality, ready-made tomato sauce or make your own favourite tomato sauce if you have the time.

Preparation time: 15 minutes Cooking time: 30 minutes

*300 g (10½ oz) packet frozen spinach,
defrosted
400 g (14 oz) fresh reduced fat ricotta cheese
¼ teaspoon ground nutmeg
2 tablespoons pine nuts, toasted
30 g (1 oz) Parmesan cheese, finely grated
4 fresh lasagne sheets
300 g (10½ oz) ready-made tomato
pasta sauce
freshly ground black pepper
torn basil leaves, to serve*

1 Preheat the oven to 180°C (350°F/Gas 4). Put the spinach in a colander and squeeze out the excess liquid.

2 Combine the ricotta, nutmeg, pine nuts and half the Parmesan in a large bowl and mix with a wooden spoon. Lay one sheet of lasagne on a flat surface and spoon a quarter of the ricotta mixture along the long edge of the sheet. Roll lengthways to make a long sausage shape and place into an oblong lasagne dish, cutting the lasagne to fit if necessary. Repeat with the remaining ricotta mixture and lasagne sheets.

3 Spoon the pasta sauce over the cannelloni and season with pepper. Cover with foil and bake for 25–30 minutes, or until the pasta is tender and the sauce is bubbling.

4 Divide the lasagne into four and serve. Spoon any extra tomato sauce over the top, sprinkle with the remaining Parmesan and scatter over the basil.

ACTIVITY TIP
Become an active person by nature where you see every moment as an opportunity for movement, not an inconvenience. In other words, be the person who offers to run an errand, wash the car or walk to the local shop. Every moment of activity counts in the long run.

G GI LOW
Per serve
1975 kJ (470 Cal), 18 g fat (saturated 8 g),
25 g protein, 49 g carbohydrate, 7 g fibre,
627 mg sodium

ADUKI BEAN STEW SERVES 4

Aduki beans are eaten widely in their native Japan. They are one of the most delicious of all dried beans and have a sweet meaty flavour. The beans are soaked overnight to shorten the cooking time.

Soaking time: Overnight Preparation time: 15 minutes Cooking time: 45–50 minutes

200 g (7 oz/1 cup) dried aduki beans, soaked overnight in water
1 leek, sliced
1 carrot, diced
1 orange sweet potato (about 250 g/9 oz), diced
1 chicken stock cube, crumbled
1 teaspoon Tabasco sauce
2 tablespoons tomato paste (purée)
1 tablespoon Worcestershire sauce
70 g (2½ oz/1 cup) small broccoli florets
15 g (½ oz/¼ cup) chopped coriander leaves
4 tablespoons low fat natural yoghurt (optional)

1 Drain the beans from the soaking water and rinse well. Put the beans in a saucepan, cover with water and bring to the boil, then reduce the heat and simmer for 30–35 minutes, partly covered (the beans should still be a little hard after this time).

2 Add all other ingredients, except the broccoli and coriander, and cook for a further 10 minutes. Add the broccoli and coriander and simmer for a further 5 minutes, or until the broccoli is tender.

3 Serve in bowls topped with a spoonful of natural yoghurt, if desired. You may like to serve this with steamed koshihikari rice or sourdough bread.

COOK'S TIP
You may need to buy dried aduki beans from a health-food store, as they are not as widely available as the canned version.

GI LOW G
Per serve
900 kJ (215 Cal), 2 g fat (saturated <1 g),
14 g protein, 32 g carbohydrate, 13 g fibre,
320 mg sodium

Recipe: Jill McMillan

BULGUR-STUFFED SNAPPER IN TOMATO ORANGE SAUCE SERVES 4

This recipe is equally good using any whole fish. The fish could also be wrapped in foil and cooked on the barbecue rather than in the oven. Preparation time: 20 minutes Cooking time: 40 minutes Chilling time: 2 hours (optional)

4 x 350 g (12 oz) small whole snapper,
cleaned and scaled

STUFFING
175 g (6 oz/1 cup) bulgur wheat
250 ml (9 fl oz/1 cup) boiling water
2 tablespoons olive oil
2 garlic cloves, finely chopped
½ red (Spanish) onion, finely diced
½ zucchini (courgette), finely diced
½ red capsicum (pepper), finely diced
4 sun-dried tomatoes, roughly chopped
½ teaspoon dried oregano
2 tablespoons finely chopped basil
1 tablespoon lemon juice
freshly ground black pepper

MARINADE
400 g (14 oz) can crushed tomatoes
zest and juice of 1 orange
½ teaspoon dried oregano
30 g (1 oz/½ cup) torn basil, plus whole
leaves, extra to serve
freshly ground black pepper

1 To prepare the stuffing, put the bulgur wheat in a bowl, cover with the boiling water and steam for about 10 minutes, or until all the water has absorbed. Meanwhile, heat the oil in a frying pan over medium heat and lightly sauté the garlic and onion for 3 minutes, or until the onion is soft. Add the zucchini and capsicum and sauté for a further 2 minutes. Add the remaining ingredients, season with pepper, then stir in the bulgur wheat and mix well to combine.

2 Stuff the fish with some of the bulgur wheat mixture, then place the fish in a large non-metallic ovenproof dish. The leftover stuffing can be served cold with the fish or reheated in the oven for 10 minutes.

3 To make the marinade, mix together all the ingredients and season with pepper. Pour the marinade over the stuffed fish. Refrigerate for 2 hours to allow the flavours to develop, or cook immediately if preferred.

4 Preheat the oven to 200°C (400°F/Gas 6). Cover the dish with foil and bake for 30–40 minutes, or until the fish is cooked through and flakes easily when tested with a fork. Garnish with the extra basil leaves. Serve the fish with the remaining bulgur wheat stuffing, and with a mixed green salad and crusty bread, if desired.

Ⓖ GI LOW
Per serve
2160 kJ (515 Cal), 15 g fat (saturated 3 g),
51 g protein, 39 g carbohydrate, 9 g fibre,
263 mg sodium

CHICKEN AND BOK CHOY STIR-FRY SERVES 4

Preparation time: 10 minutes Cooking time: 10 minutes

300 g (10½ oz) dried egg noodles
2 teaspoons peanut oil
2 garlic cloves, finely chopped
2 tablespoons grated ginger
2 skinless chicken breast fillets (about
240 g/8½ oz each), cut into thin strips
leaves and stems from 3 heads bok choy
(pak choy), roughly chopped
90 g (3 oz) baby corn, halved
3 tablespoons soy sauce
1 tablespoon oyster sauce
1 red chilli, seeded and thinly sliced
80 g (2¾ oz/½ cup) cashew nuts, toasted
4 spring onions, thinly sliced

1 Cook the noodles in plenty of boiling water for 4–5 minutes. Rinse in cold water, drain well and set aside.

2 Heat the oil in a wok and add the garlic and ginger. Stir-fry for a few seconds, or until aromatic, then add the chicken and stir-fry for 5 minutes, or until the chicken changes colour. Add the bok choy and corn and stir until the bok choy is wilted, then add the soy sauce, oyster sauce and chilli. Stir to coat the chicken in the sauce. Add the noodles and toss to heat through. Serve in bowls and scatter over the cashews and spring onions.

GI LOW Ⓖ

Per serve
2540 kJ (605 Cal), 20 g fat (saturated 4 g),
42 g protein, 63 g carbohydrate, 5 g fibre,
1318 mg sodium

Recipe: Lynne Mullins, Noodles to Pasta

BEEF AND NOODLES WITH CHILLI JAM SERVES 4

Preparation time: 10 minutes Cooking time: 15 minutes

2 tablespoons peanut oil
80 g (2¾ oz/½ cup) cashew nuts
500 g (1 lb 2 oz) beef rump steak,
thinly sliced
200 g (7 oz) Thai chilli jam
150 g (5¼ oz) green beans, trimmed and cut
into 3 cm (1¼ in) pieces
125 g (4½ oz) baby corn, halved
25 g (1 oz/½ cup) chopped coriander leaves
500 g (1 lb 2 oz) packet fresh Asian noodles,
such as Hokkien (egg) noodles

1 Heat 1 teaspoon of the oil in a wok or frying pan over medium heat. Stir-fry the cashews for 1–2 minutes, or until brown. Remove and set aside.

2 Heat the remaining oil in the wok. Stir-fry the beef, in batches, for about 3 minutes each batch, or until brown. Return all the beef to the wok, then add the chilli jam, beans, corn and 60 ml (2 fl oz/¼ cup) water. Stir-fry for 4 minutes, or until the vegetables are tender. Stir in the coriander and cashew nuts. Add the noodles to the wok and stir to combine. Heat through and serve.

GI LOW Ⓖ

Per serve
2874 kJ (684 Cal), 32 g fat (saturated 9 g),
37 g protein, 61 g carbohydrate, 7 g fibre,
390 mg sodium

Left: Beef and noodles with chilli jam

PASTA WITH SCALLOPS AND WILD ROCKET SERVES 4–6

Wild rocket has a stronger flavour than ordinary rocket and is perfect for salads with shaved Parmesan. Here the rocket's piquant, cress-like bite complements the richness of the scallops. Preparation time: 10 minutes Cooking time: 15 minutes

350 g (12 oz) dried pasta, such as spaghetti
or linguine
2 tablespoons extra-virgin olive oil
2 garlic cloves, finely chopped
1 red chilli, seeded and finely chopped
400 g (14 oz) fresh scallops, cleaned and
prepared, halved if large
3 Roma (plum) tomatoes, peeled and chopped
juice of 1 lemon
35 g (1¼ oz/1 cup firmly packed) wild
rocket leaves
freshly ground black pepper

1 Bring a large saucepan of water to the boil and cook the pasta until al dente.

2 Meanwhile, heat the oil in a large, deep frying pan or large saucepan over medium heat. Add the garlic and chilli and cook, stirring, for 1–2 minutes, being careful that the garlic does not brown. Add the scallops and cook for 1–2 minutes on each side, or until just golden. Stir in the tomatoes and lemon juice and cook for a further minute.

3 When the pasta is cooked, drain it thoroughly, then add to the sauce along with the rocket leaves. Season with pepper, then lightly toss the ingredients together to heat through. Serve immediately.

COOK'S TIP
To peel tomatoes, first remove the stems, then score a cross in the bottom of each tomato using a knife. Blanch the tomatoes in boiling water for 30–60 seconds. Transfer to a bowl of cold water, then peel the skin away from the cross.

G GI LOW
Per serve (4)
1850 kJ (440 Cal), 11 g fat (saturated 2 g),
22 g protein, 62 g carbohydrate, 4 g fibre,
175 mg sodium

CHAR-GRILLED STEAK WITH CHILLI CORN SALSA SERVES 2

This versatile corn salsa is delicious served with steaks, such as eye fillet or rump, and complements other meats too, including thinly sliced rare roast beef and barbecued chicken sausages. Preparation time: 10 minutes Cooking time: 12–15 minutes

2 x 100 g (3½ oz) small lean beef steaks
150 g (5¼ oz/1 bunch) rocket leaves

CHILLI CORN SALSA
2 corn cobs
1 tomato, seeded and cut into small dice
½ red (Spanish) onion, finely chopped
2 small red chillies, seeded, finely chopped
10 g (¼ oz/½ bunch) chives, finely chopped
45 g (1½ oz/½ bunch) coriander, leaves
picked and finely chopped
2 tablespoons balsamic vinegar
2 tablespoons extra-virgin olive oil

1 To make the chilli corn salsa, put the corn cobs in a saucepan of boiling water and cook for 5 minutes. Drain. Use a sharp knife to cut the kernels from the cobs, then place them in a large bowl. Add the tomato, onion, chillies, half the chives and half the coriander.

2 Whisk together the vinegar and oil and toss through the salsa.

3 Char-grill or barbecue the steaks to your liking. To serve, put a steak on each plate, spoon a small mound of salsa on each steak and serve with the rocket. Garnish with the remaining herbs.

GI LOW G

Per serve
2070 kJ (495 Cal), 26 g fat (saturated 5 g),
31 g protein, 30 g carbohydrate, 10 g fibre,
83 mg sodium

Chilli corn salsa recipe: Luke Mangan

PORK VINDALOO SERVES 4

Vindaloo curries are renowned for their heat, but if you like your vindaloo fiery, add an extra green chilli or two. Serve with steamed basmati rice and your favourite curry accompaniments.

Marinating time: 1 hour Preparation time: 30 minutes Cooking time: 1½ hours

750 g (1 lb 10 oz) diced pork
2 tablespoons olive oil
2 onions, thinly sliced
4 garlic cloves, thinly sliced
4 cm (1½ in) piece ginger, cut into matchsticks
3 ripe tomatoes, diced
2 green chillies, seeds removed, chopped
1 teaspoon soft brown sugar
25 g (1 oz/½ cup) chopped coriander leaves

VINDALOO MARINADE
2 tablespoons vindaloo curry powder (page 162, or ready-made), or to taste
4 tablespoons white wine vinegar
1 tablespoon malt vinegar

350 g (12 oz/2 cups) steamed basmati rice, to serve
mung bean dhal (page 164), to serve (optional)
cucumber raita (page 162), to serve (optional)

1 To make the vindaloo marinade, combine the curry powder and vinegars together in a large non-metallic bowl and mix well.

2 Add the pork to the bowl and toss to coat in the marinade. Cover and leave to marinate in the refrigerator for 1 hour (or more if you have the time).

3 Heat the oil in a flameproof casserole dish over low heat and gently cook the onions until soft and golden. Add the garlic, ginger, tomatoes, chillies and sugar and stir well to combine. Add the pork (reserve the marinade), increase the heat and cook for 1–2 minutes, or until the meat is starting to brown. Add 250 ml (9 fl oz/1 cup) water and the reserved marinade, cover and simmer for about 1–1½ hours, stirring occasionally, or until the meat is very tender (the cooking time depends on the size of the diced pork). Stir in the coriander just before serving.

4 Serve the curry with the steamed rice, and with accompaniments such as mung bean dhal and cucumber raita, if desired.

COOK'S TIPS

You can make the vindaloo marinade yourself or, if short on time, you can substitute this for about 125 g (4½ oz/½ cup) good-quality ready-made vindaloo paste.

To obtain 350 g (12 oz/2 cups) cooked rice you will need 140 g (5 oz/⅔ cup) raw rice.

GI MEDIUM
Per serve (includes ½ cup rice)
1905 kJ (455 Cal), 14 g fat (saturated 2 g),
46 g protein, 34 g carbohydrate, 4 g fibre,
250 mg sodium

Recipe: Carol Selva Rajah, Gourmet Asian Cuisine

BARBECUED FISH TIKKA MAKES 4 SKEWERS

Here the fish and vegetables are threaded onto long metal skewers and then marinated in a spicy yoghurt mixture. Traditionally, the tikka is cooked in an Indian clay tandoor oven, which gives them a wonderful smoky flavour, but you can cook your skewers on the barbecue. Preparation time: 20 minutes Marinating time: 30 minutes Cooking time: 10 minutes

FISH SKEWERS
*400 g (14 oz) firm white fish steaks,
cut into 16 x 2.5 cm (1 in) chunks
1 large red (Spanish) onion, cut into 8 wedges
1/2 red capsicum (pepper), cut into
6 x 2.5 cm (1 in) squares
1/2 green capsicum (pepper), cut into
6 x 2.5 cm (1 in) squares*

YOGHURT MARINADE
*200 g (7 oz) low fat natural yoghurt
1/2 onion, finely chopped
2 teaspoons finely grated ginger
2 garlic cloves, crushed
1 teaspoon ground coriander
2 tablespoons lemon juice
1 tablespoon garam masala
1 teaspoon paprika
1 teaspoon chilli powder, or to taste
2 tablespoons tomato paste (purée)*

*4 lemon wedges
saffron pilaf (page 163), to serve (optional)
cucumber raita (page 162), to serve (optional)
mung bean dhal (page 164), to serve
(optional)*

1 To make the yoghurt marinade, combine all the ingredients in a non-metallic bowl and mix well.

2 To make the fish skewers, allow 4 fish chunks, 2 onion wedges and 3 squares of capsicum (a mix of red and green look good) for each skewer. Thread the fish chunks, onion wedges and capsicum squares onto the skewers in the following order: capsicum, fish, onion, fish, capsicum, fish, onion, fish, capsicum. Place in a shallow dish that is long enough to hold the skewers. Coat the skewers with the marinade mixture, cover, and refrigerate for 30 minutes to allow the flavours to develop.

3 Heat a barbecue or char-grill pan and cook the fish skewers for about 5 minutes on each side, or until the fish is cooked through and the vegetables are slightly charred on the edges.

4 Serve the fish skewers with lemon wedges for squeezing over. You may also like to serve with accompaniments such as saffron pilaf, cucumber raita and mung bean dhal.

GI LOW Ⓖ
Per serve (2 fish skewers)
1960 kJ (470 Cal), 9 g fat (saturated 2 g),
34 g protein, 60 g carbohydrate, 4 g fibre,
500 mg sodium

Recipe: Carol Selva Rajah, Gourmet Asian Cuisine

SLOW-ROAST LAMB WITH CHICKPEAS SERVES 4

This recipe is perfect for a dinner party or family get-together, as everything can be prepared in advance and pulled from the oven when you are ready to eat. Potatoes are usually served with a roast but unnecessary here, as a chickpea and tomato sauce provides the starchy accompaniment. Preparation time: 15 minutes Cooking time: 2½–3 hours

4 large garlic cloves, crushed
1 teaspoon ground cumin
2 tablespoons olive oil
juice of 1 lemon
freshly ground black pepper
1 kg (2 lb 4 oz) leg of lamb, large areas
of visible fat removed
2 onions, chopped
250 ml (9 fl oz/1 cup) vegetable stock
4 tablespoons tomato paste (purée)
400 g (14 oz) can chopped tomatoes
1 cinnamon stick
¼ teaspoon ground cloves
1 tablespoon pure floral honey
400 g (14 oz) can chickpeas,
rinsed and drained

1 Preheat the oven to 170°C (325°F/Gas 3). Put the garlic, cumin, oil and lemon juice in a bowl, season with pepper, and mix to combine. Rub this mixture over the lamb.

2 Put the lamb in a large, non-stick ovenproof casserole dish over medium heat and brown the lamb on all sides. Remove from the dish and set aside.

3 Add the onions to the hot dish and fry for 4–5 minutes, or until soft and translucent. Add the stock, tomato paste, tomatoes, cinnamon, cloves and honey and mix well. Return the lamb to the dish and spoon over the sauce. Cover with a well-fitting lid or foil and roast in the oven for 2½–3 hours. Remove the lamb, set aside and keep warm, then return the dish to the stovetop. Add the chickpeas and heat through.

4 Slice the lamb and serve with the chickpea tomato sauce spooned over the top. Serve with steamed green vegetables, if desired.

ACTIVITY TIP
A balanced exercise program, including aerobic, resistance and stretching exercise, will give you the best results. Variety is also important because the body becomes efficient at anything it does repeatedly, so after a while you'll need to add something new to your exercise program.

G GI LOW

Per serve (3 slices of lamb)
1500 kJ (360 Cal), 15 g fat (saturated 5 g),
30 g protein, 25 g carbohydrate, 7 g fibre,
440 mg sodium

BARLEY RISOTTO WITH TROUT SERVES 4

Barley is one of the oldest cultivated cereals and has one of the lowest GI values of any food. It's also versatile: add pearl barley to soups and stews, fuel your day with barley porridge or make a barley risotto—all great ways to reduce the overall GI of a meal.
Preparation time: 15 minutes Cooking time: 1 hour

1 tablespoon olive oil
1 onion, finely chopped
2 large garlic cloves, finely chopped
2 large field mushrooms (about 200 g/7 oz in total), chopped into bite-sized chunks
220 g (7³/₄ oz/1 cup) pearl barley
2 tablespoons barbecue sauce
500 ml (17 fl oz/2 cups) hot vegetable stock
freshly ground black pepper
4 x 150 g (5¹/₄ oz) trout fillets
juice of ¹/₂ lemon
1 tablespoon chopped dill
lemon wedges, to serve (optional)

1 Preheat the oven to 180°C (350°F/Gas 4). Heat the oil in a flameproof casserole dish over medium heat and sauté the onion and garlic for about 3 minutes, or until soft. Add the mushrooms and cook for 1 minute, then add the barley, barbecue sauce and hot stock. Stir well and season with pepper.

2 Cover with the lid and bake for 40–45 minutes. After this time, place the trout fillets on top of the risotto, squeeze over the lemon juice and season with pepper. Replace the lid and cook for a further 15 minutes.

3 Flake the trout into large pieces and gently combine with the barley risotto. Sprinkle with the dill and serve with lemon wedges, for squeezing over, if desired. Serve with either a green salad or steamed green vegetables.

COOK'S TIP
To reduce the cooking time, cover the barley with water in the morning and leave to soak for the day.

GI LOW **G**
Per serve
1910 kJ (455 Cal), 13 g fat (saturated 3 g),
43 g protein, 37 g carbohydrate, 8 g fibre,
180 mg sodium

ROASTED PUMPKIN AND MUSHROOM LASAGNE SERVES 8

Soft layers of pumpkin, sweet potato and mushrooms, and a creamy ricotta sauce make this lasagne a memorable meal to share with family and friends. Preparation time: 30 minutes Cooking time: 1 hour

*400 g (14 oz) pumpkin, cut into
1 cm (½ in) cubes
400 g (14 oz) orange sweet potato, cut into
1 cm (½ in) cubes
2 large sprigs rosemary
3 garlic cloves, crushed
freshly ground black pepper
olive oil spray
1 litre (35 fl oz/4 cups) skim milk
1 large onion, sliced
3 heaped tablespoons plain flour
250 g (9 oz) ricotta cheese
250 g (9 oz) lasagne sheets
200 g (7 oz) mushrooms, sliced
1 spring onion, sliced
50 g (1¾ oz) reduced fat cheddar
cheese, grated*

1 Preheat the oven to 200°C (400°F/Gas 6). Mix the pumpkin, sweet potato, rosemary and garlic in a bowl and season with pepper. Lightly spray a baking tray with olive oil, put the vegetables on the tray and bake for 20 minutes, or until tender.

2 Put the milk and onion in a saucepan over medium heat. Heat until just below boiling point, then turn off the heat and sit for 10 minutes. Mix the flour with a little water, then add to the milk, bring to a simmer and cook for 5 minutes, then add the ricotta cheese.

3 Spray a lasagne dish with olive oil. Add a layer of lasagne sheets, then a quarter of the sauce, a quarter of the baked pumpkin and sweet potato and a quarter of the mushrooms and spring onion. Continue until all the lasagne sheets, vegetables and sauce are used (you will end up with four layers). Sprinkle with grated cheese.

4 Bake for 35–45 minutes, or until cooked through and golden on top. Rest for 5 minutes before cutting. Serve with a mixed green salad, if desired.

Ⓖ GI LOW
Per serve
1245 kJ (300 Cal), 5 g fat (saturated 3 g),
18 g protein, 44 g carbohydrate, 4 g fibre,
177 mg sodium

Recipe: Michelle Trute, Cooking with Conscience

MARINATED STEAKS WITH MEXICAN BEAN SALAD SERVES 4

Game meats, such as ostrich, kangaroo or venison, are a perfect choice, being incredibly lean and packed with essential nutrients, including iron and zinc. Soaking time: Overnight Marinating time: 1–2 hours Preparation time: 10 minutes Cooking time: 45–50 minutes

4 x 150 g (5¼ oz) lean steaks, such as ostrich or kangaroo
8 asparagus spears, trimmed
1 tablespoon Bourbon whisky

MARINADE
125 ml (4 fl oz/½ cup) red wine
2 teaspoons liquid hickory smoke sauce
1 tablespoon olive oil
1 tablespoon soy sauce
½ teaspoon paprika
freshly ground black pepper

MEXICAN BEAN SALAD
300 g (10½ oz/1½ cups) black beans, soaked overnight in water
1 red chilli, finely diced
3 spring onions, thinly sliced
½ red capsicum (pepper), finely diced
cayenne pepper, to taste
1 tablespoon extra-virgin olive oil

1 To make the marinade, combine all the ingredients in a bowl and season with pepper. Put the steaks in a plastic bag and pour in the marinade. Squeeze out the excess air and seal the bag. Marinate at room temperature for 1–2 hours, turning the steaks occasionally.

2 To make the Mexican bean salad, put the beans in a saucepan, cover with water and bring to the boil. Cook for 30–40 minutes, or until al dente (cooking time will vary depending on the size of the beans and their soaking time). Transfer to a bowl and allow to cool, then add the remaining salad ingredients. Cover and set aside.

3 Heat a char-grill pan or frying pan until quite hot and grill the asparagus for 2–3 minutes, or until slightly browned. Remove and set aside.

4 Remove the steaks from the marinade, reserving the marinade, and pat dry with paper towels. Cook on the char-grill for about 3 minutes on each side. Lean meat should be served rare to medium-rare (overcooking the meat will leave it tough and dry).

5 Put the reserved marinade in a small saucepan and add the Bourbon. Heat gently and simmer for 4–5 minutes to reduce and thicken the sauce. To serve, spoon a little of the sauce over the steaks and serve with the warm Mexican bean salad and grilled asparagus.

GI LOW Ⓖ
Per serve
1925 kJ (460 Cal), 12 g fat (saturated 2 g),
50 g protein, 31 g carbohydrate, 15 g fibre,
250 mg sodium

Recipe: Steffan Rössner

BAKED SALMON WITH MIXED BEAN SALSA SERVES 4

In a traditional Mediterranean diet, fish would be included once or twice a week. We now know that eating fish regularly will help reduce the risk of heart disease, so aim for two or three serves a week. Preparation time: 15 minutes Cooking time: 20–30 minutes

4 salmon fillets
1 lemon, halved
90 g (3 oz/1 bunch) coriander, leaves
picked and chopped
freshly ground black pepper

MIXED BEAN SALSA
440 g (15½ oz) can four-bean mix,
rinsed and drained
1 tablespoon chopped black olives
6 sun-dried tomatoes, chopped
1 red chilli, finely chopped (remove the seeds
for a milder taste)
1 small red (Spanish) onion, finely chopped
1 tablespoon olive oil
2 teaspoons balsamic vinegar

GREEN SALAD
1 tablespoon olive oil
2 teaspoons balsamic vinegar
1 teaspoon Dijon mustard
1 teaspoon pure floral honey
150–200 g (5¼–7 oz) mixed salad leaves

1 Preheat the oven to 180°C (350°F/Gas 4). Put the salmon fillets in an ovenproof dish, squeeze over the lemon juice, sprinkle over half of the coriander leaves and season with plenty of pepper. Cover with foil and bake for 20–30 minutes for medium to well-done (or bake for about 15 minutes if you prefer your salmon rare).

2 Meanwhile, to make the mixed bean salsa, combine all the ingredients in a bowl. Add the remaining coriander and mix well.

3 To make a dressing for the green salad, put the oil, vinegar, mustard and honey in a screw-top jar and shake to combine. Drizzle over the salad leaves.

4 Place the salmon fillets on each plate, top with a generous spoonful of the bean salsa and serve with the green salad.

Ⓖ GI LOW
Per serve
1949 kJ (464 Cal), 24 g fat (saturated 5 g),
45 g protein, 15 g carbohydrate, 6 g fibre,
360 mg sodium

CHICKEN PASTA WITH CARAMELISED ONIONS SERVES 4–6

It's worth taking the time to roast the capsicum (pepper) and remove its skin before adding it to the pasta, as this makes it sweeter (the skin can be a little bitter). Preparation time: 15 minutes Cooking time: 35 minutes

2 tablespoons olive oil
2 red (Spanish) onions, peeled and cut into thin wedges
2 teaspoons sugar
1 red capsicum (pepper)
2 chicken breast fillets (about 300 g/10½ oz in total), thinly sliced
4 spring onions, sliced
2 teaspoons crushed garlic
250 ml (9 fl oz/1 cup) low fat evaporated milk
250 ml (9 fl oz/1 cup) chicken stock
2 tablespoons sun-dried tomato pesto or tomato paste (purée)
350 g (12 oz) dried pasta, such as spirals or penne
30 g (1 oz/½ cup) shredded basil
freshly ground black pepper

1 To make the caramelised onions, heat 1 tablespoon of the oil in a frying pan and add the onions and sugar. Cook over medium–low heat, stirring occasionally, for 10 minutes, or until the onions are soft and golden brown. Take care to keep the heat low enough so the onions do not burn. Remove to a bowl and cover to keep warm.

2 Cut the capsicum into quarters lengthways and remove the seeds and stalk. Lay the pieces, skin-side up, on a baking tray lined with baking paper. Place under a hot grill and cook for about 7 minutes, or until the skin is blackened and blistered. Using tongs, place the hot pieces of capsicum in a plastic freezer bag. Twist to seal and put aside to cool slightly. When cool, remove the skin and slice the flesh into strips.

3 Meanwhile, heat the remaining tablespoon of oil in a large frying pan. Add the chicken and cook for 4–5 minutes, or until the chicken is browned and cooked through. Add the spring onions and garlic and cook for a further minute. Stir in the evaporated milk, stock, pesto and capsicum strips. Bring to the boil, then reduce the heat and simmer for 1–2 minutes. Remove the chicken mixture to a bowl and cover to keep warm.

4 Cook the pasta in a large saucepan of boiling water until al dente. When the pasta is cooked, drain it and return to the saucepan. Stir in the chicken mixture and caramelised onion and heat through. Stir in the basil and season with pepper.

GI LOW Ⓖ
Per serve (6)
1650 kJ (390 Cal), 10 g fat (saturated 2 g),
23 g protein, 50 g carbohydrate, 4 g fibre,
260 mg sodium

STEAMED MONKFISH WITH GARLIC CHIVES AND GINGER SERVES 2

Rick Stein says Chinese seafood cooking is some of the best in the world. To make it even more authentic, we have used a bamboo steamer, or you could steam the fish in a frying pan. Preparation time: 15 minutes Cooking time: 5 minutes

350–400 g (12–14 oz) monkfish fillet, or other skinless, white firm-fleshed fish
¼ teaspoon salt
½ tablespoon very finely shredded ginger
70 g (2½ oz/1 small bunch) garlic chives,
4 leaves wild garlic, or 1 garlic clove, cut into fine shreds
1 tablespoon sesame oil
1 tablespoon dark soy sauce
2 spring onions, thinly sliced on the diagonal
350 g (12 oz/2 cups) steamed basmati rice, to serve

1 Lightly season the fish fillet with salt and then cut the fillet across into thin slices. Arrange the slices in a single layer on a heatproof plate and scatter over the ginger.

2 To steam the fish, place a trivet in a wide, shallow frying pan, add 1 cm (½ in) of water and bring to the boil. Rest the plate on the trivet, cover the pan with the lid and steam for 2–3 minutes, or until the fish is almost cooked. Alternatively, if you have a bamboo steamer, put the fish on the plate and place in the steamer. Cover with the lid. Bring a large saucepan or wok filled with water to the boil. Place the steamer over the top and steam the fish for 2–3 minutes.

3 Scatter the garlic chives, wild garlic or shredded garlic over the fish and steam, covered, for a further minute. Meanwhile, put the sesame oil and soy sauce in a small saucepan and heat briefly.

4 Remove the fish from the pan or steamer and pour away half the cooking juices. Scatter over the spring onions, then pour over the hot sesame oil and soy mixture. Serve with steamed rice.

G GI MEDIUM
Per serve (includes 1 cup rice)
2080 kJ (500 Cal), 12 g fat (saturated 2 g),
43 g protein, 54 g carbohydrate, 2 g fibre,
1140 mg sodium

Rick Stein is not only a celebrity chef but also runs four restaurants, a delicatessen, a patisserie, a seafood cookery school and a 33-bedroom hotel in the small fishing port of Padstow, in Cornwall. In addition to this, he has produced his well-known TV cookery series, Taste of the Sea, and has written nine cookery books. Rick is also very interested in diet, particularly in the healthy properties of fish and the vital role that omega 3 plays in our diet. And, he says, what our grandmothers told us is true—fish is good for the brain.

CHICKEN TAGINE WITH SWEET POTATO, CARROTS AND PRUNES SERVES 4

The combination of ginger, cinnamon, prunes and honey gives this tagine that taste of Morocco. Serve this one-pot meal with a crispy salad and bread to mop up the juices. Preparation time: 15 minutes Cooking time: 45–50 minutes

1 tablespoon olive oil
20 baby onions (bite-sized)
2 orange sweet potatoes (about 750 g/
1 lb 10 oz in total), cut into
bite-sized chunks
2 carrots, cut into bite-sized chunks
1 tablespoon grated ginger
12 pitted prunes
1 teaspoon ground cinnamon
1 teaspoon pure floral honey
375 ml (13 fl oz/1½ cups) vegetable or
chicken stock
freshly ground black pepper
4 chicken breast fillets (about 600 g/1 lb 5 oz
in total), skin and visible fat
removed, cut into quarters
2 tablespoons chopped coriander leaves
2 tablespoons chopped mint

1 Preheat the oven to 180°C (350°F/Gas 4). Heat the oil in a large flameproof casserole dish over low heat, add the onions and cook for 5 minutes, or until the onions are soft and golden. Add the sweet potatoes, carrots and ginger and cook for a further 5 minutes, or until the vegetables start to colour a little.

2 Stir in the prunes, cinnamon and honey. Allow to heat through, then pour in the stock and season with pepper. Lay the chicken pieces in the liquid, then cover the dish and cook in the oven for 35–40 minutes, or until the chicken is cooked through. Stir in the coriander and mint and serve.

ACTIVITY TIP
Dancing in some form has always been important for humans all around the globe. Find a class close to you, hit the local nightspot or simply throw on your favourite CD at home and get moving!

GI LOW Ⓖ
Per serve
1930 kJ (460 Cal), 13 g fat (saturated 3 g),
38 g protein, 47 g carbohydrate, 8 g fibre,
140 mg sodium

SWEET POTATOES IN GINGER, CAYENNE AND PEANUT SAUCE SERVES 4–6

Savour the flavour of this robust vegetarian dish and serve with a side dish of basmati rice, or as the carb accompaniment to meat or fish. Preparation time: 20 minutes Cooking time: 45 minutes

1 tablespoon olive oil
1 large onion, cubed
4 garlic cloves, crushed
5 cm (2 in) piece ginger, finely grated
3 small sweet potatoes (about 850 g/1 lb 14 oz in total), cubed
450 g (1 lb) white cabbage, cubed
2 teaspoons paprika
1 teaspoon cayenne pepper
440 g (15½ oz) can diced Roma (plum) tomatoes
250 ml (9 fl oz/1 cup) pineapple juice
125 g (4½ oz/½ cup) smooth peanut butter
freshly ground black pepper
1 carrot, grated
1 raw beetroot, grated
1 banana, sliced
juice of 1 lime
2 tablespoons chopped coriander leaves
steamed low GI rice, to serve (optional)

1 Heat the oil in a large heavy-based saucepan over medium heat and sauté the onion, garlic and ginger for 2 minutes, then add the sweet potatoes and cabbage. When the vegetables start to soften, add the paprika and cayenne. Stir to coat the vegetables in the spices. Add the tomatoes and pineapple juice. Cover and simmer for 35–40 minutes, or until the vegetables are soft.

2 Stir in the peanut butter until well combined, adding a little water if it is too thick. Season with pepper, then transfer to serving bowls.

3 Toss the carrot, beetroot and banana in the lime juice and scatter over the vegetables. Garnish with coriander and serve with steamed low GI rice, if desired.

G GI LOW
Per Serve (6)
1490 kJ (355 Cal), 17 g fat (saturated 3 g),
13 g protein, 39 g carbohydrate, 11 g fibre,
155 mg sodium

Recipe: Chris and Carolyn Caldicott, World Food Café

CRUNCHY-TOPPED LENTIL LOAF SERVES 4–6

Lentils are one of nature's superfoods—rich in protein, fibre and B vitamins. All colours and types have a similar low GI. Serve this lentil loaf with a spicy home made tomato salsa, or pack and take on a picnic.

Preparation time: 20 minutes Cooking time: 1¼ hours

90 g (3 oz/⅓ cup) red lentils
90 g (3 oz/½ cup) green lentils
375 ml (13 fl oz/1½ cups) chicken stock
1 bay leaf
1 teaspoon olive oil
1 onion, finely chopped
1 garlic clove, crushed
125 g (4½ oz) mushrooms, finely chopped
½ red capsicum (pepper), finely chopped
½ yellow capsicum (pepper), finely chopped
125 g (4½ oz/1½ cups loosely packed) fresh wholegrain breadcrumbs
2 tablespoons chopped coriander leaves
zest and juice of ½ lemon
2 eggs, lightly beaten
freshly ground black pepper

1 Wash the lentils and put into a large saucepan with the stock and bay leaf. Bring to the boil, then reduce the heat and simmer for 20–30 minutes, or until the lentils are soft and all the fluid has absorbed.

2 Preheat the oven to 180°C (350°F/Gas 4). Line a loaf tin with non-stick baking paper.

3 Heat the oil in a saucepan or large deep frying pan and sauté the onion and garlic for 2 minutes, or until the onion is soft. Add the mushrooms and capsicums and cook for a further 2 minutes. Remove the bay leaf and add the lentil mixture to the pan, along with the breadcrumbs (reserving about 3 tablespoons of the breadcrumbs), coriander, lemon zest and juice, and the beaten egg. Season with pepper and mix well. The mixture should be soft, but not runny.

4 Spoon the lentils into the prepared tin, sprinkle the reserved breadcrumbs over the top, and bake for 35–40 minutes, or until firm to the touch. Remove from the oven and allow to cool in the tin for 10 minutes before turning out.

5 Serve hot or cold in thick slices with your favourite bought or home-made tomato salsa (see spicy tomato salsa, page 30), and a mixed green salad.

GI LOW Ⓖ
Per serve (6)
695 kJ (165 Cal), 4 g fat (saturated 1 g),
12 g protein, 19 g carbohydrate, 6 g fibre,
222 mg sodium

Recipe: Isobel McMillan

ROAST LAMB AND VEGETABLES WITH THYME AND ROSEMARY SERVES 6

This is your traditional roast with a flavoursome, and healthy, Mediterranean twist. Roasting vegetables brings out their natural sweetness and is an easy way of serving a great array. Preparation time: 20 minutes Chilling time: 6 hours or overnight Cooking time: 1 hour

2 tablespoons roughly chopped thyme
3 tablespoons olive oil
1 kg (2 lb 4 oz) boneless piece of lamb, such
as boned leg or loin
5 sprigs thyme, each sprig broken into
3 pieces
3 sweet potatoes (about 1.2 kg/2 lb 12 oz
in total), cut into 3 cm (1¼ in) chunks
6 zucchini (courgettes) (about 500 g/
1 lb 2 oz), cut in half lengthways
3 large red (Spanish) onions, each cut into
8 wedges
1 red capsicum (pepper), cut lengthways
into 12 slices
3 sprigs rosemary
3 garlic cloves, each cut into 5 slices
2 tablespoons lemon juice

1 Combine the chopped thyme and 1 tablespoon of the oil in a small bowl. Put the lamb into a large glass or ceramic dish and use your hands to coat the lamb in the thyme mixture.

2 Roll up the lamb and tie with kitchen string to keep the shape and ensure the lamb cooks evenly. Then, using a sharp knife, cut 15 evenly spaced slits, about 2 cm (¾ in) deep and 1 cm (½ in) long, into the top of the lamb. Insert a sprig of thyme into each slit. Cover with plastic wrap and refrigerate for at least 6 hours or overnight.

3 Preheat the oven to 180°C (350°F/Gas 4). Put all the vegetables together in a large roasting tin and scatter over the leaves from the rosemary. Drizzle with 1 tablespoon of the oil and toss gently to coat. Place the lamb on top of the vegetables. Insert a slice of garlic into each slit with the thyme.

4 Put the lemon juice and the remaining tablespoon of oil in a screw-top jar and shake to combine. Drizzle over the lamb. Roast in the oven, basting with the pan juices occasionally, for 50 minutes (rare) or 60 minutes (medium). Turn off the oven. Transfer the lamb to a plate, cover with foil and set aside for 10 minutes to rest. Return the vegetables to the oven to keep warm until the lamb is ready to be sliced and served.

G GI LOW
Per serve
2045 kJ (490 Cal), 19 g fat (saturated 6 g),
40 g protein, 37 g carbohydrate, 7 g fibre,
125 mg sodium

PORK WITH HONEY GLAZED APPLES SERVES 2

Lentils gently simmered in stock until they are mushy make a delicious low GI mash for all sorts of meaty mains and are very quick and easy to prepare.

Preparation time: 15 minutes Cooking time: 40–45 minutes

olive oil spray
2 x 200 g (7 oz) pork loin steaks, butterfly steaks or medallions
2 teaspoons margarine
2 teaspoons olive oil
2 green apples, cored and cut into 5 mm (¼ in) thick slices
1 tablespoon pure floral honey
1 tablespoon lemon juice
200 g (7 oz) steamed green beans, to serve

RED LENTIL MASH
160 g (5½ oz/⅔ cup) split red lentils
1 bay leaf
250 ml (9 fl oz/1 cup) vegetable stock

1 Spray a non-stick frying pan with olive oil and heat over medium–high heat. Add the pork to the pan and cook for 4–5 minutes each side, or until lightly browned and cooked to your liking. Transfer to a plate and cover to keep warm.

2 Add the margarine and oil to the pan and reduce the heat to medium–low. Add the apple slices and cook for about 7 minutes, stirring and turning occasionally, until the apples begin to brown. Add the honey and lemon juice and stir to coat the apples. Cook for a further 2 minutes.

3 To make the red lentil mash, put the lentils and bay leaf in a saucepan and add the stock. Bring to the boil, then reduce to a simmer and cook for 20–25 minutes, stirring occasionally (add extra water if the mixture becomes too dry). Cook until the lentils are soft and mushy.

4 Serve a scoop of the lentil mash on individual plates, top with the pork and apples and drizzle over the pan juices. Serve with steamed green beans.

ACTIVITY TIP
Research has shown that just 30 minutes of moderate intensity exercise each day can help to improve your health. If you prefer, you can break this down to two sessions of 15 minutes, or even three sessions of 10 minutes, and you will still see some benefits.

GI LOW Ⓖ
Per serve
2520 kJ (600 Cal), 14 g fat (saturated 3 g),
63 g protein, 57 g carbohydrate, 15 g fibre,
540 mg sodium

BEEF FAJITAS SERVES 4

This recipe makes enough for three rolls for each person. Serve the fajitas accompanied with your choice of grated cheese, shredded lettuce, guacamole, yoghurt, tomato salsa and refried beans.

Preparation time: 15 minutes Cooking time: 15 minutes

2 tablespoons olive oil
500 g (1 lb 2 oz) rump steak, thinly sliced
1 red (Spanish) onion, sliced
1 red capsicum (pepper), sliced
1 yellow capsicum (pepper), sliced
1–2 jalapeño chillies, seeded and finely chopped
½ teaspoon chilli powder
2 teaspoons sweet paprika
1 teaspoon ground cumin
1 teaspoon ground coriander
juice of 1 lime
2 tablespoons tomato paste (purée)
2 tablespoons chopped coriander leaves
12 soft flour tortillas

1 Heat the oil in a large frying pan over medium heat. Cook the beef, in batches, for 3–4 minutes each batch, or until brown. Remove and set aside.

2 Add the onion, capsicums and chillies and cook for a further 3 minutes. Stir in the chilli powder, paprika, cumin, ground coriander, lime juice and tomato paste. Return all the meat to the pan and cook for 2–3 minutes, or until heated through. Stir in the coriander leaves.

3 Heat the tortillas following the packet instructions, either in the microwave for 30 seconds, or wrap in foil and warm in the oven for a few minutes. Spoon a portion of the beef mixture onto a plate with a tortilla. To eat, place some of the beef mixture on one side of a tortilla, add accompaniments of your choice, and roll up.

G GI LOW

Per serve (3 fajitas)
2485 kJ (590 Cal), 22 g fat (saturated 4 g),
38 g protein, 58 g carbohydrate, 5 g fibre,
610 mg sodium

CHICKEN BREASTS WITH LENTIL MASH SERVES 4

These chicken breasts are stuffed with a creamy mix of feta cheese, spinach and semi-dried tomatoes and served on spicy lentil mash with a mixed green salad to make a meal where everyone will be coming back for more ...

Preparation time: 20 minutes Cooking time: 1 hour

4 chicken breast fillets (about 600 g/1 lb 5 oz in total), skin and visible fat removed

STUFFING
100 g (3½ oz) baby spinach leaves
40 g (1½ oz/¼ cup) semi-dried (sun-blushed) tomatoes
50 g (1¾ oz) reduced fat feta cheese
1 tablespoon low fat cream cheese
freshly ground black pepper

GREEN LENTIL MASH
185 g (6½ oz/1 cup) green lentils
¼ teaspoon ground turmeric
1 tablespoon olive oil
1 onion, finely chopped
2 garlic cloves, finely chopped
juice of ½ lemon
freshly ground black pepper

1 To make a stuffing for the chicken, put the spinach, semi-dried tomatoes, feta cheese and cream cheese in the bowl of a food processor. Season with pepper, then roughly blend. Be careful not to overprocess; the mixture should be quite coarse.

2 Preheat the oven to 200°C (400°F/Gas 6). Slice open the chicken breasts lengthways to create a pocket. Fill the pockets with the stuffing. Place the chicken in an ovenproof dish, cover with foil and bake for 30 minutes, or until cooked through and golden brown.

3 Meanwhile, to make the green lentil mash, put the lentils in a saucepan over medium heat, cover with water, and add the turmeric. Bring to the boil, then reduce the heat to a simmer and cook, partly covered, for about 30 minutes, or until the lentils are soft.

4 Towards the end of cooking, heat the oil in a saucepan and fry the onion and garlic for 3–4 minutes, or until the onion is soft. Add the lentils, lemon juice and season with plenty of pepper.

5 Serve the lentil mash topped with the stuffed chicken breast. Serve with a mixed green salad or steamed vegetables.

GI LOW Ⓖ
Per serve
1830 kJ (435 Cal), 17 g fat (saturated 5 g),
49 g protein, 21 g carbohydrate, 8 g fibre,
260 mg sodium

DESSERTS AND SWEET TREATS

BEING ON A LOW GI DIET DOESN'T MEAN WE HAVE TO SKIP DESSERT. IN FACT, MANY OF THE INGREDIENTS USED IN DESSERTS, SUCH AS FRUIT AND DAIRY PRODUCTS, HAVE A LOW GI. THEY MAKE A VALUABLE CONTRIBUTION TO OUR FRUIT AND DAIRY INTAKE AND, BEING CARBOHYDRATE-RICH, ADD TO OUR FEELING OF FULLNESS.

HONEY BANANA CUPS SERVES 2

Preparation time: 5 minutes

200 g (7 oz) low fat honey-flavoured yoghurt
1 large banana, just ripe, peeled and sliced
2 passionfruit
2 coconut macaroons

1 Spoon the yoghurt into two small cups, dividing evenly between them. Divide the banana between the two cups and spoon the passionfruit over the top. Serve a coconut macaroon alongside.

COOK'S TIP

Unlike most other fruit, bananas contain both sugars and starch. The less ripe the banana, the lower its GI. As the banana ripens, the starch turns to sugars and the GI increases.

Ⓖ GI LOW

Per serve
800 kJ (190 Cal), 3 g fat (saturated 2 g),
8 g protein, 31 g carbohydrate, 5 g fibre,
105 mg sodium

ITALIAN STRAWBERRIES SERVES 4

Preparation time: 5 minutes

500 g (1 lb 2 oz/3⅓ cups) strawberries, sliced
2 tablespoons balsamic vinegar
2 tablespoons sugar
small mint leaves, to garnish
8 scoops low fat ice-cream or frozen yoghurt, to serve

1 Place the strawberries in a bowl. Pour over the vinegar, sprinkle with the sugar and toss to combine. Divide the strawberries between four bowls and garnish with the mint leaves. Serve with a couple of scoops of ice-cream or frozen yoghurt.

Ⓖ GI LOW

Per serve
503 kJ (120 Cal), 2 g fat (saturated 1 g),
4 g protein, 21 g carbohydrate, 3 g fibre,
41 mg sodium

Recipe: Steffan Rössner

Right: Honey banana cups

FRESH PLUM AND RICOTTA STRUDEL SERVES 6

Plums and other blue-red fruit, such as cherries, blueberries and cranberries, are rich in a particular type of anti-oxidant known as anthocyanins. Here's a low-fat version of the strudel Catherine Saxelby makes, but using plums instead of apples.

Preparation time: 20 minutes Cooking time: 45 minutes

30 g (1 oz) polyunsaturated or monounsaturated margarine
40 g (1½ oz/½ cup) fresh wholemeal breadcrumbs
80 g (2¾ oz/⅓ cup) soft brown sugar
½ teaspoon ground cinnamon
6 plums (about 250 g/9 oz) or 425 g (15 oz) can plums, drained well
6 sheets filo pastry
olive oil spray
125 g (4½ oz) reduced fat ricotta cheese

1 Melt the margarine in a saucepan over medium heat. Add the breadcrumbs and sugar, reserving 2 teaspoons sugar, and cook for 15 minutes, stirring to break up any lumps. Remove from the heat and stir in the cinnamon. Allow to cool.

2 Halve the plums, remove the stones, and thinly slice the flesh.

3 Preheat the oven to 190°C (375°F/Gas 5). Lightly grease a baking tray. Lay two sheets of filo pastry on top of each another. Spray the top sheet with olive oil, then sprinkle over one-third of the crumb mixture. Top with two more filo sheets, spray the top sheet with oil, then sprinkle over another third of the crumbs. Top with the remaining two sheets, spray with oil, then sprinkle over the remaining crumbs.

4 Spread the ricotta along the edge of the pastry. Arrange the plums on top and sprinkle with the reserved sugar. Roll up the pastry, as for a Swiss roll, tucking in the edges as you roll. Carefully transfer the roll to the prepared baking tray. Spray the top with oil and bake for 10 minutes, then reduce the heat to 180°C (350°F/Gas 4) and bake for 20 minutes, or until the pastry is crisp and brown. Serve warm with low fat vanilla ice-cream, if desired.

Catherine Saxelby is Australia's most dynamic nutritionist and food commentator who understands the demands of today's busy world and the complexity of food issues. The author of seven books, she is also Nutrition Editor for *Table* magazine and has written many articles on all aspects of food, fat loss and special diets in a career spanning 20 years.

GI LOW Ⓖ
Per serve
865 kJ (205 Cal), 6 g fat (saturated 2 g),
5 g protein, 30 g carbohydrate, 3 g fibre,
260 mg sodium

CHOCOLATE APPLE SAUCE CUPCAKES MAKES 18

These cupcakes are light, moist and very delicious. Although the estimated GI is medium, they have a relatively small amount of carbohydrate per cake. They are also low in saturated fat, which makes them a good choice as an occasional indulgence.
Preparation time: 15 minutes Cooking time: 25 minutes

125 g (4½ oz) reduced fat margarine or butter
170 g (6 oz/¾ cup) caster sugar
2 eggs
60 g (2 oz/½ cup) cocoa powder
400 g (14 oz/1½ cups) ready-made apple sauce
260 g (9¼ oz/1¾ cups) wholemeal flour
1 teaspoon baking powder
1 teaspoon bicarbonate of soda
½ teaspoon salt

1 Preheat the oven to 180°C (350°F/Gas 4). Grease and flour 18 holes of two 12-hole cupcake trays or muffin tins.

2 Cream the margarine and sugar in a deep mixing bowl with electric beaters for 1–2 minutes, or until pale. Add the eggs and cocoa powder and mix until smooth. Fold in the apple sauce.

3 Combine the flour, baking powder, bicarbonate of soda and the salt in a small mixing bowl. Stir the dry ingredients into the egg mixture and gently mix to combine; do not overmix.

4 Spoon the mixture into the prepared holes, filling each one half to three-quarters full with the mixture. Bake for 22–25 minutes, or until cooked through. Cool a little before removing the cakes from the trays.

Ⓖ GI MEDIUM
Per serve
590 kJ (140 Cal), 5 g fat (saturated 1 g),
3 g protein, 21 g carbohydrate, 2 g fibre,
150 mg sodium

Recipe: Johanna Burani

SYRUPY ORANGES WITH YOGHURT SERVES 2

So the only fruit you have is oranges? You can still make a delicious dessert. Not only that, you'll also be boosting your fruit intake and enjoying all the health benefits of a single orange.

Preparation time: 10 minutes Cooking time: 15 minutes

juice of 1 orange
2 tablespoons sugar
2 large oranges, peeled, pith removed
1 tablespoon brandy or Cointreau™ liqueur (optional)
100 g (3½ oz) peach and passionfruit frozen yoghurt
4 slices almond bread

1 Combine the orange juice, sugar and 60 ml (2 fl oz/¼ cup) water in a frying pan. Stir over medium heat until the sugar dissolves. Reduce the heat to low and simmer, without stirring, for 10–12 minutes to reduce the syrup.

2 Cut the peeled oranges into slices about 1 cm (½ in) thick and add to the syrup in the pan. Add the brandy or liqueur, bring to a simmer and cook for 3 minutes.

3 Spoon the oranges into bowls and pour over the syrup. Top with a scoop of frozen yoghurt and serve with the almond bread.

COOK'S TIP
Almond bread is a very thin, slightly sweet crispbread containing whole almonds. It is available in the biscuit or gourmet section of supermarkets.

GI LOW Ⓖ
Per serve
1250 kJ (300 Cal), 4 g fat (saturated 2 g),
6 g protein, 55 g carbohydrate, 4 g fibre,
38 mg sodium

CHOCOLATE MOUSSE WITH BERRIES SERVES 6

This is a delectable version of a traditionally high-fat favourite. It can be made up to 2 days ahead and is very easy to prepare. For the best results, use a good-quality cocoa powder.

Preparation time: 10 minutes Cooking time: 5 minutes Chilling time: 2–3 hours

30 g (1 oz/¼ cup) cocoa powder
2 teaspoons gelatine powder
110 g (3¾ oz/½ cup) sugar
375 ml (13 fl oz/1½ cups) skim evaporated milk
125 ml (4 fl oz/½ cup) reduced fat cream
150 g (5¼ oz/1 cup) strawberries or raspberries, to serve
6 scoops low fat ice-cream (optional)

1 Sift the cocoa into a saucepan, then stir in the gelatine and sugar. Stir in about 60 ml (2 fl oz/¼ cup) of the milk, stirring to form a smooth paste. Put the saucepan over medium heat and stir for about 3 minutes to dissolve the sugar and gelatine, then gradually stir in the remaining milk. Heat until the liquid is hot but not boiling, stirring occasionally.

2 Remove from the heat, stir in the cream, then divide the mixture between six 125 ml (4 fl oz/½ cup) glasses or ramekins. Chill until set.

3 Serve with the fresh berries and with a scoop of ice-cream, if desired.

ACTIVITY TIP

Working with a personal trainer can be a great way to improve your health and fitness. A good trainer will design an exercise program tailored to your needs and fitness level, as well as provide motivation and support. Many trainers now offer services for a reasonable rate and you can choose to use a health club or train at home or outdoors.

G GI LOW
Per serve
790 kJ (190 Cal), 5 g fat (saturated 3 g),
8 g protein, 28 g carbohydrate, 2 g fibre,
90 mg sodium

FRUIT SOUFFLE SERVES 4

This soufflé is made with semolina, which has a low GI of 55. Semolina is a coarse grain made from the first millings of the creamy yellow endosperm from wheat grain (the finer grain, when milled from durum wheat, is used to make pasta). Here the semolina is cooked with low GI fruit to make a delicious, hot soufflé. Preparation time: 15 minutes Cooking time: 30 minutes

450 g (1 lb) mixed fresh fruit, such as apples,
rhubarb and/or berries
2 tablespoons soft brown sugar
625 ml (21 fl oz/2½ cups) skim milk
5 tablespoons semolina
1 egg, separated
ground nutmeg

1 Preheat the oven to 180°C (350°F/Gas 4). Chop the fruit (except if using berries) and place in a saucepan with 1 tablespoon of the sugar and 60 ml (2 fl oz/¼ cup) water. Bring to the boil, then reduce the heat, cover and simmer for 5–10 minutes, or until the fruit is soft. Spoon the fruit into a 1.25 litre (44 fl oz/5 cups) ovenproof dish or into four 250 ml (9 fl oz/1 cup) soufflé dishes.

2 Put the milk in a saucepan and heat until just coming to the boil. Sprinkle the semolina and the remaining sugar over the milk. Cook, stirring, until the mixture thickens, then continue to cook for 1 minute. Remove the pan from the heat, stir in the egg yolk and allow to cool slightly.

3 Whisk the egg white until stiff peaks form, then fold into the semolina. Spoon the semolina mixture over the fruit and sprinkle with the nutmeg. Bake for 20 minutes, or until the soufflé has risen and is golden. Serve hot.

GI LOW Ⓖ
Per serve
770 kJ (180 Cal), 2 g fat (saturated 0 g),
10 g protein, 32 g carbohydrate, 3 g fibre,
91 mg sodium

APRICOT OAT MUNCHIES MAKES ABOUT 24

Need a quick snack between meals? Then make a batch of these delicious apricot and oat munchies. Store in an airtight container and use for school lunches, or bake these healthy cookies for fundraisers and fetes.

Preparation time: 15 minutes Cooking time: 12–15 minutes

180 g (6¼ oz/1 cup) dried apricots, chopped
80 ml (2½ fl oz/⅓ cup) boiling water
100 g (3½ oz/1 cup) rolled oats
125 g (4½ oz/1 cup) plain flour, sifted
75 g (2½ oz/½ cup) oat bran
115 g (4 oz/½ cup) soft brown sugar
60 g (2 oz/½ cup) chopped walnuts
½ teaspoon baking powder
½ teaspoon ground cinnamon
½ teaspoon ground nutmeg
2 egg whites
3 tablespoons olive oil

1 Preheat the oven to 180°C (350°F/Gas 4). Lightly grease two baking trays. Put the apricots in a bowl, pour over the boiling water and leave to soak for 10 minutes. Allow the mixture to cool.

2 Combine the oats, flour, oat bran, sugar, walnuts, baking powder and spices in a large bowl.

3 Beat the egg whites until stiff peaks form, fold into the cooled apricot mixture, then add the oil. Mix into the dry ingredients.

4 Drop spoonfuls of the mixture onto the prepared baking trays, then bake for 12–15 minutes, or until light brown. Leave for 5 minutes before lifting off the tray and placing on a wire rack to cool. Store in an airtight container.

Ⓖ GI MEDIUM

Per serve (1 cookie)
465 kJ (110 Cal), 5 g fat (saturated <1 g),
3 g protein, 14 g carbohydrate, 2 g fibre,
13 mg sodium

Recipe: Catherine Saxelby, Eating for the Healthy Heart

PEARS POACHED IN CHAMPAGNE SERVES 4

This elegant, light dessert makes the perfect ending to a meal. Although vanilla beans are a little expensive, the wonderful fragrance and flavour that they impart to the poaching syrup is unsurpassed. If preferred, substitute the vanilla bean with 1 teaspoon pure, or natural, vanilla essence. Preparation time: 10 minutes Cooking time: 35 minutes

*375 ml (13 fl oz/1½ cups) Champagne
or sparkling white wine
125 ml (4 fl oz/½ cup) orange juice
115 g (4 oz/½ cup) caster sugar
1 vanilla bean, split
4 firm pears, peeled, quartered and cored*

1 Combine the Champagne, orange juice, sugar, vanilla bean and 250 ml (9 fl oz/1 cup) water in a large saucepan. Stir until the sugar dissolves, then bring to the boil and simmer for 5 minutes.

2 Add the pears to the syrup and continue to simmer for 20–30 minutes, or until the pears are tender (the cooking time will vary according to how ripe the pears are). Leave to cool in the syrup. When cool, spoon into small bowls. Serve with a spoonful of low fat yoghurt, if desired.

COOK'S TIP
Vanilla beans are readily available from specialty spice and food shops and larger supermarkets. A good bean is dark brown or black, slightly moist to touch, as pliable as a piece of licorice and immediately fragrant. You should be able to wrap a vanilla bean tightly around your finger—if you can't, then it's too dry.

GI LOW Ⓖ
Per serve
1070 kJ (255 Cal), trace fat (saturated 0 g),
<1 g protein, 51 g carbohydrate, 3 g fibre,
14 mg sodium

SCOTTISH OATCAKES MAKES 35

Traditional oatcakes are made using lard or butter, both full of the saturated fats that we are recommending you cut down on. This recipe uses an unsaturated table spread instead of butter and the result is an equally delicious but altogether healthier oatcake.
Preparation time: 15 minutes Chilling time: 20 minutes Cooking time: 15–20 minutes

170 g (6 oz/1⅓ cups) coarse oatmeal
75 g (2½ oz/½ cup) wholemeal self-raising flour, plus extra for dusting
¼ teaspoon sea salt
100 g (3½ oz) unsaturated margarine, chilled
2 tablespoons chilled water

TOPPINGS
low fat ricotta cheese
sliced strawberries, or slices of fresh or dried figs

1 Combine the oatmeal, flour, sea salt and margarine in the bowl of a food processor and process until the mixture resembles coarse breadcrumbs, then slowly add the chilled water until the mixture forms a stiff dough. Stop at this point, even if you haven't used all of the water.

2 Put the dough in a plastic bag and in the freezer for about 20 minutes. Preheat the oven to 180°C (350°F/Gas 4).

3 Remove the dough from the bag and roll out on a floured board to 3 mm (⅛ in) thick. Cut into rounds about 4 cm (1½ in) in diameter, place on a non-stick baking tray and bake for 15–20 minutes, or until golden. Transfer to a wire rack to cool.

4 To make the topping for the oatcakes, put a teaspoon of ricotta on each and top with either a sliced strawberry or a slice of fig.

COOK'S TIPS

Scottish oatcakes are also a delicious substitute for bread when served with soups and salads. Cut them into slightly larger rounds, about 6 cm (2½ in) in diameter, if serving with soup.

In Australia, oatmeal may be hard to find, but persevere and ask your local health-food or wholefood store to source it for you.

G GI LOW
Per serve (2 oatcakes)
350 kJ (85 Cal), 4 g fat (saturated 1 g),
2 g protein, 9 g carbohydrate, 1 g fibre,
71 mg sodium

G GI LOW
Per serve (with toppings)
450 kJ (100 Cal), 6 g fat (saturated 1.5 g),
3 g protein, 12 g carbohydrate, 2 g fibre,
82 mg sodium

Recipe: Judy Davie, The Food Coach

APPLE AND STRAWBERRY CRUMBLE SERVES 4

Crumbles are real comfort food. Making the 'crumble' with rolled oats keeps the GI low and the fibre high, and the strawberries are rich in vitamin C and protective anti-oxidants.

Preparation time: 20 minutes Cooking time: 15 minutes

3 cooking apples, such as Granny Smiths, peeled, cored and sliced
2 tablespoons pure floral honey
250 g (9 oz/1²/₃ cups) strawberries, hulled and halved
100 g (3¹/₂ oz/1 cup) rolled oats
2 tablespoons soft brown sugar
¹/₂ teaspoon ground cinnamon
2 tablespoons reduced fat margarine, melted

1 Preheat the oven to 200°C (400°F/Gas 6). Lightly grease a 1 litre (35 fl oz/ 4 cups) ovenproof dish with margarine.

2 Put the apples, honey and 2 tablespoons water in a saucepan. Bring to the boil, then reduce the heat to low, cover and simmer for 3–4 minutes, or until the apples have softened a little. Remove from the heat and stir in the strawberries. Spoon the mixture into the prepared dish.

3 Put the oats in a food processor and process until the mixture is coarse. Combine the oats in a bowl with the sugar, cinnamon and margarine. Mix together and spoon evenly over the fruit.

4 Bake for 15–20 minutes, or until the crumble is crisp and golden. Serve with low fat vanilla ice-cream or custard, if desired.

ACTIVITY TIP
Develop an after dinner walking habit with your partner or a good friend.

GI LOW Ⓖ
Per serve
1180 kJ (280 Cal), 8 g fat (saturated 1 g),
4 g protein, 48 g carbohydrate, 5 g fibre,
45 mg sodium

CHERRY OAT CRUNCHIES MAKES 42

Who doesn't love cookies? How about cookies that your body will love too? Add them to packed lunches, or serve with a glass of milk after school or in the evening.

Preparation time: 15 minutes Cooking time: 15 minutes

olive oil spray
55 g (2 oz/¼ cup) soft brown sugar
90 g (3 oz/¼ cup) pure floral honey
125 g (4½ oz) reduced fat margarine
or butter
2 eggs
½ teaspoon bicarbonate of soda
½ tablespoon vanilla essence
150 g (5¼ oz/1 cup) wholemeal flour
200 g (7 oz/2 cups) rolled oats
20 fresh cherries, pitted and roughly chopped
60 g (2 oz/½ cup) roughly chopped walnuts
80 g (2¾ oz/2 cups) bran flakes cereal,
crushed

1 Preheat the oven to 180°C (350°F/Gas 4). Lightly spray two baking trays with olive oil.

2 Put the sugar, honey, margarine, eggs, bicarbonate of soda and vanilla essence in a large mixing bowl. Beat on medium speed for 2 minutes. Fold in the flour, oats, cherries, walnuts and bran flakes. Mix thoroughly.

3 Drop spoonfuls of the mixture onto the prepared baking trays, spacing them about 5 cm (2 in) apart. Bake for 15 minutes, or until light brown. Leave for 5 minutes before lifting off the tray and placing on a wire rack to cool. Store in an airtight container.

COOK'S TIP
Instead of cherries, you can try other fresh fruit in season such as berries, or substitute with 90 g (3 oz/½ cup) chopped dried apricots.

G GI LOW
Per serve (2 cookies)
650 kJ (155 Cal), 7 g fat (saturated 1 g),
3 g protein, 19 g carbohydrate, 2 g fibre,
65 mg sodium

Recipe: Johanna Burani

BERRY AND VANILLA CREME DESSERT SERVES 4

This is a delicious, simple dessert that can be made with fresh berries in summer—strawberries, blueberries and blackberries—or frozen berries when they are out of season. Berries not only have a low GI but are also incredibly rich in disease-fighting anti-oxidants.
Preparation time: 15 minutes Marinating time: 15 minutes

juice of 1 orange
1 tablespoon soft brown sugar
1 tablespoon sweet wine
250 g (9 oz/1¼ cups) mixed fresh or frozen berries
8 sponge finger biscuits (savoiardi)

VANILLA CREME
100 g (3½ oz) low fat cream cheese, at room temperature
4 tablespoons low fat sour cream
4 teaspoons icing sugar
1 teaspoon vanilla essence

1 To make the vanilla crème, put the cream cheese and sour cream in a mixing bowl and stir with a wooden spoon to combine. Sift in the icing sugar, add the vanilla essence and stir well to combine.

2 Combine the orange juice, sugar and wine in a bowl, then add the berries and leave to marinate for 15 minutes.

3 Choose four 250 ml (9 fl oz/1 cup) glasses with a wide base. Cut a sponge finger biscuit to cover the base of each glass. Add a spoonful of berries and a drizzle of marinade over the biscuit base, then top with a spoonful of vanilla crème. Top with another layer of sponge finger, the berries, a little more marinade, and finish with the vanilla crème. Chill until ready to serve.

GI LOW Ⓖ
Per serve
960 kJ (230 Cal), 10 g fat (saturated 6 g),
6 g protein, 27 g carbohydrate, 4 g fibre,
160 mg sodium

GRAPEFRUIT GRANITA SERVES 6

This refreshing, citrusy granita is light and flavoursome and the perfect end to a heavy or spicy meal. To allow adequate time for the granita to freeze, it is best to prepare this recipe a day ahead.

Preparation time: 5 minutes Cooking time: 5 minutes Freezing time: 5¹/₂ hours

110 g (3³/₄ oz/¹/₂ cup) sugar
2 whole star anise
625 ml (21 fl oz/2¹/₂ cups) fresh pink grapefruit juice

1 Put 80 ml (2¹/₂ fl oz/¹/₃ cup) water in a saucepan, add the sugar and star anise and bring to the boil over medium heat, stirring occasionally, until the sugar has dissolved. Discard the star anise and allow the sugar syrup to cool to room temperature.

2 Put the grapefruit juice in a bowl and stir in the cooled sugar syrup. Pour the mixture into a 32 x 23 cm (13 x 9 in) baking dish. Cover tightly with plastic wrap, put the dish in the freezer and freeze for about 45 minutes, or until the mixture is icy around the edge of the dish. Using a fork, scrape the edges to distribute the frozen portions evenly. Cover and freeze again for another 45 minutes, or until the mixture is icy around the edges and the overall texture is slushy. Use the fork to distribute the frozen portions evenly. Cover and return to the freezer for about 3 hours, or until frozen solid.

3 Remove from the freezer. Using a fork, scrape the granita down the length of the pan, forming icy flakes. Return to the freezer for at least 1 hour, for the final freezing. To serve, scoop the flaked granita into tall goblets or parfait glasses. When served, the granita should look like a fluffy pile of dry pink crystals.

G GI LOW

Per serve
420 kJ (100 Cal), 0 g fat (saturated 0 g),
<1 g protein, 25 g carbohydrate, 0 g fibre,
5 mg sodium

Recipe: Emma Pemberton

BASIC RECIPES

CHERMOULA SPICE MIX

½ onion, finely chopped
1 teaspoon finely chopped coriander leaves
2 teaspoons finely chopped parsley
1 garlic clove, crushed
3 teaspoons ground cumin
2 teaspoons mild paprika
1 teaspoon turmeric
pinch of cayenne pepper
salt and freshly ground black pepper

1 Combine all the ingredients and set aside to allow the flavours to develop. Use as a rub for meat or poultry before roasting or barbecuing.

MAKES ABOUT ⅓ CUP

Recipe: Liz and Ian Hemphill, Herbies Spices

VINDALOO CURRY POWDER

6 teaspoons medium-heat chilli powder (or use mild or hot, according to taste)
4 teaspoons white poppy seeds
3 teaspoons ground cumin
2 teaspoons mild paprika
1 teaspoon ground cassia
1 teaspoon ground ginger
½ teaspoon amchur powder
½ teaspoon freshly ground black pepper
¼ teaspoon ground cloves
pinch ground star anise

1 Combine all the ingredients and mix thoroughly. Store in an airtight container.

MAKES ABOUT ⅔ CUP

Recipe: Liz and Ian Hemphill, Herbies Spices

HARISSA

10 teaspoons chopped, dried red chillies or dried chilli flakes
3 teaspoons crushed garlic
3 teaspoons sweet paprika
2 teaspoons caraway seeds
2 teaspoons coriander seeds
1 teaspoon cumin seeds, dry-roasted
1 teaspoon salt
6 spearmint leaves, finely chopped
3 teaspoons olive oil

1 Soak the chillies in 10 teaspoons (50 ml/1¾ fl oz) hot water for 15 minutes (do not drain off the water).

2 Crush the remaining ingredients (except the oil) using a mortar and pestle, then add to the soaked chillies in the bowl. Mix to combine. Add the oil, a little at a time, mixing to form a thick paste (you may not need to use all of the oil). Store, covered, in the refrigerator and use within 4 weeks. This Tunisian harissa blend is fairly fiery, so use with caution.

MAKES ABOUT ½ CUP

Recipe: Liz and Ian Hemphill, Herbies Spices

CUCUMBER RAITA

200 g (7 oz) low fat natural yoghurt
1 small Lebanese (short) cucumber, peeled and seeded, finely chopped
45 g (1½ oz/½ bunch) coriander, leaves picked and chopped

1 Combine all the ingredients in a serving bowl. Cover and refrigerate until needed.

MAKES ABOUT 1 CUP

Recipe: Carol Selva Rajah, Gourmet Asian Cuisine

HOMMOUS

400 g (14 oz) can chickpeas, drained (liquid reserved)
135 g (4³/4 oz/¹/2 cup) tahini
2 garlic cloves, finely chopped
juice of 1 lemon
¹/4 teaspoon salt and freshly ground black pepper, to taste

1 Combine all the ingredients in a food processor and blend, adding just enough of the reserved chickpea liquid to make a smooth paste. Serve in a bowl. Garnish with a drizzle of olive oil, chopped parsley, pine nuts and a sprinkle of paprika, if desired.

MAKES 2 CUPS

G GI LOW
Per serve (¹/4 cup)
590 kJ (140 Cal), 11 g fat (saturated 1 g), 6 g protein,
5 g carbohydrate, 4 g fibre, 345 mg sodium

TABBOULI

175 g (6 oz/1 cup) bulgur wheat
30 g (1 oz/1 cup) finely chopped flat-leaf (Italian) parsley
4 small spring onions, finely chopped
1 tomato, finely chopped
2 tablespoons lemon juice
2 tablespoons olive oil
¹/4 teaspoon salt and freshly ground black pepper

1 Put the bulgur wheat in a bowl, cover with boiling water and soak for 20–30 minutes. Drain well and roll the grains in a clean, lint-free kitchen towel to squeeze out the excess water. Combine the bulgur wheat, parsley, spring onions and tomato in a bowl.

2 Combine the lemon juice, oil, salt and pepper in a screw-top jar and shake well. Pour over the tabbouli and toss lightly to combine. Tabbouli will keep for 2 days, covered, in the refrigerator.

SERVES 4

G GI LOW
Per serve
1106 kJ (263 Cal), 10 g fat (saturated 1 g), 6 g protein,
33 g carbohydrate, 8 g fibre, 175 mg sodium

SAFFRON PILAF

300 g (10¹/2 oz/1¹/2 cups) basmati rice
¹/2 teaspoon saffron threads
1 tablespoon boiling water
1 tablespoon olive oil
3 spring onions, sliced
¹/2 red capsicum (pepper), diced
2 garlic cloves, crushed
625 ml (21 fl oz/2¹/2 cups) chicken stock
80 g (2³/4 oz/¹/2 cup) frozen peas, defrosted
30 g (1 oz/¹/4 cup) sultanas
30 g (1 oz/¹/4 cup) slivered almonds, toasted

1 Rinse the rice under cold water. Drain and set aside. Place the saffron threads in a small bowl and pour over the boiling water. Set aside to allow the colour to infuse.

2 Heat the oil in a large saucepan. Cook the spring onions, capsicum and garlic for 2 minutes. Add the rice, stock, saffron and its soaking water, and bring to the boil. Reduce the heat to low, cover and simmer for 10–12 minutes, stirring from time to time, or until the rice is just tender.

3 Remove from the heat and stir in the peas, sultanas and almonds. Cover and set aside for 5 minutes before serving.

SERVES 4–6

G GI MEDIUM
Per serve (6)
1140 kJ (270 Cal), 6 g fat (saturated <1 g), 6 g protein,
48 g carbohydrate, 2 g fibre, 265 mg sodium

BAKED BEETROOT SALAD

2 large beetroot (about 500 g/1 lb 2 oz in total)
2 tablespoons lemon juice
1 tablespoon olive oil
1/4 teaspoon salt and freshly ground black pepper
2 tablespoons finely chopped flat-leaf (Italian) parsley

1 Preheat the oven to 180°C (350°F/Gas 4). Leaving the beetroot unpeeled and with 3 cm (1 1/4 in) of root attached (so they don't 'bleed' during cooking), wrap in foil. Place the beetroot on a baking tray and bake for 45 minutes, or until cooked (test with a skewer). When cool, peel the beetroot; the skins will slip off easily. Finely dice or grate the beetroot and spoon into a serving dish.

2 Combine the lemon juice, oil, salt and pepper in a screw-top jar and shake well. Pour the dressing over the beetroot and stir to combine. Serve garnished with the parsley.

SERVES 4

Ⓖ GI MEDIUM

Per serve
430 kJ (102 Cal), 5 g fat (saturated <1 g), 3 g protein,
11 g carbohydrate, 4 g fibre, 220 mg sodium

MUNG BEAN DHAL

180 g (6 1/4 oz/1 cup) dried whole mung beans
1/4 teaspoon turmeric
1/2 teaspoon salt
1 tablespoon olive oil
1/2 onion, chopped
2 garlic cloves, finely chopped
1–2 green chillies, finely chopped (remove the seeds for a milder taste)
90 g (3 oz/1 bunch) coriander, leaves picked and chopped

1 Cover the mung beans with 875 ml (30 fl oz/ 3 1/2 cups) water and bring to the boil. Reduce the heat, add the turmeric and simmer for 40–50 minutes, or until the beans are tender. Add the salt and turn off the heat.

2 Heat the oil in a small non-stick frying pan over medium heat and sauté the onion and garlic until brown. Add the chillies and fry for 30 seconds, then tip the onion and garlic into the saucepan with the mung beans. Cover with the lid and allow the flavours to develop. Before serving, stir in the coriander.

SERVES 4

Ⓖ GI LOW

Per serve
845 kJ (200 Cal), 5 g fat (saturated <1 g), 11 g protein,
29 g carbohydrate, 8 g fibre, 300 mg sodium

Recipe: Isobel McMillan

YOUR LOW GI DIET FOODS

To make easy low GI choices, you'll need to stock the right foods. Here are ideas for what to keep in your pantry, refrigerator and freezer. These foods have optimum flavour and nutritional value and can all feature, in moderation, in a low GI diet.

WHAT TO KEEP IN YOUR PANTRY

ASIAN SAUCES Hoi sin, oyster, soy and fish sauces are a good basic range.

BARLEY One of the oldest cultivated cereals, barley is very nutritious and high in soluble fibre. Look for products such as pearl barley to use in soups, stews and pilafs.

BLACK PEPPER Buy freshly ground pepper or grind your own peppercorns.

BREAD Low GI options include grainy, stoneground wholemeal, pumpernickel, sourdough, English-style muffins, flat bread and pita bread.

BREAKFAST CEREALS These include traditional rolled oats, natural muesli and low GI packaged breakfast cereals.

BULGUR WHEAT Use it to make tabbouli, or add to vegetable burgers, stuffings, soups and stews.

CANNED EVAPORATED SKIM MILK This makes an excellent substitution for cream in pasta sauces.

CANNED FISH Keep a good stock of canned tuna packed in spring water, and canned sardines and salmon.

CANNED FRUIT Have a variety of canned fruit on hand, including peaches, pears, apples and nectarines—choose the brands labelled with 'no added sugar' fruit juice syrup.

CANNED VEGETABLES Sweet corn kernels and tomatoes can help to boost the vegetable content of a meal. Tomatoes, in particular, can be used freely because they are rich in anti-oxidants, as well as having a low GI.

COUSCOUS Ready in minutes, serve with casseroles and braised dishes.

CURRY PASTES A tablespoon or so makes a delicious curry base.

DRIED FRUIT These include sultanas, apricots, raisins, prunes and apples.

DRIED HERBS Oregano, basil, ground coriander, thyme and rosemary can be useful to have on stand-by in the pantry.

HONEY Try to avoid the commercial honeys or honey blends, and use the Australian 'pure floral' honeys. These varieties have a much lower GI, and include Yellowbox and Red Gum. Bioactive components in these honeys appear to reduce their GI naturally.

JAM A dollop of good-quality jam (with no added sugar) on toast contains fewer kilojoules than butter or margarine.

LEGUMES Stock a variety of legumes (dried or canned), including lentils, split peas and beans. There are many bean varieties, including cannellini, butter, borlotti, kidney and soy beans.

MUSTARD Seeded or wholegrain mustard is useful as a sandwich spread, and in salad dressings and sauces.

NOODLES Many Asian noodles such as Hokkien, udon and rice vermicelli have low to intermediate GI values because of their dense texture, whether they are made from wheat or rice flour.

NUTS Try a handful of nuts (about 30 g/ 1 oz) every other day. Try them sprinkled over your breakfast cereal, salad or dessert, and enjoy unsalted nuts as a snack as well.

OILS Try olive oil for general use; some extra-virgin olive oil for salad dressings, marinades and dishes that benefit from its flavour; and sesame oil for Asian-style stir-fries. Canola or olive oil cooking sprays are handy too.

PASTA A great source of carbohydrates and B vitamins. Fresh or dried, the preparation is easy. Simply cook in boiling water until just tender, or al dente, drain and top with your favourite sauce and a sprinkle of Parmesan cheese.

QUINOA This wholegrain cooks in about 10–15 minutes and has a slightly chewy texture. It can be used as a substitute for rice, couscous or bulgur wheat. It is very important to rinse the grains thoroughly before cooking.

RICE Basmati, Doongara or Japanese koshihikari varieties are good choices because they have a lower GI than, for example, Jasmine rice.

ROLLED OATS Besides their use in porridge, oats can be added to cakes, biscuits, breads and desserts.

SEA SALT Use in moderation.

SPICES Most spices, including ground cumin, turmeric, cinnamon, paprika and nutmeg, should be bought in small quantities because they lose pungency with age and incorrect storage.

STOCK Make your own stock or buy ready-made products, which are available in long-life cartons in the supermarket. To keep the sodium content down with ready-made stocks, look out for a low salt option.

TOMATO PASTE Use in soups, sauces and casseroles.

VINEGAR White wine or red wine vinegar and balsamic vinegar are excellent as vinaigrette dressings in salads.

WHAT TO KEEP IN YOUR REFRIGERATOR

BACON Bacon is a valuable ingredient in many dishes because of the flavour it offers. You can make a little bacon go a long way by trimming off all fat and chopping it finely. Lean ham is often a more economical and leaner way to go. In casseroles and soups, a ham or bacon bone imparts a fine flavour without much fat.

BOTTLED VEGETABLES Sun-dried tomatoes, olives, char-grilled eggplant (aubergine) and capsicum (pepper) are handy to keep as flavoursome additions to pastas and sandwiches.

CAPERS, OLIVES AND ANCHOVIES These can be bought in jars and kept in the refrigerator once opened. They are a tasty (but salty) addition to pasta dishes, salads and pizzas.

CHEESE Any reduced fat cheese is great to keep handy in the refrigerator. A block of Parmesan is indispensable and will keep for up to 1 month. Reduced fat cottage and ricotta cheeses have a short life so are best bought as needed, and they can be a good alternative to butter or margarine in a sandwich.

CONDIMENTS Keep jars of minced garlic, chilli or ginger in the refrigerator to spice up your cooking in an instant.

EGGS To enhance your intake of omega-3 fats, we suggest using omega-3-enriched eggs. Although the yoke is high in cholesterol, the fat in eggs is predominantly monounsaturated, and therefore considered a 'good fat'.

FISH Try a variety of fresh fish.

FRESH HERBS These are available in most supermarkets and there really is no substitute for the flavour they impart. For variety, try parsley, basil, mint, chives and coriander.

FRESH FRUIT Almost all fruit make an excellent low GI snack. When in season, try fruit such as apples, oranges, pears, grapes, grapefruit, peaches, apricots, strawberries and mangoes.

MEAT AND CHICKEN Lean varieties are better—try lean beef, lamb fillets, pork fillets, chicken (breast or drumsticks) and minced beef.

MILK Skim or low fat milk is best, or try low fat calcium-enriched soy milk.

VEGETABLES Keep a variety of seasonal vegetables on hand such as spinach, broccoli, cauliflower, Asian greens, asparagus, zucchini (courgette) and mushrooms. Capsicum (pepper), spring onions and sprouts (mung bean and snowpea sprouts) are great to bulk up a salad. Sweet corn, sweet potato and yam are essential to your low GI food store.

YOGHURT Low fat natural yoghurt provides the most calcium for the fewest calories. Have vanilla or fruit versions as a dessert, or use natural yoghurt as a condiment in savoury dishes. However, if using yoghurt in a hot meal, make sure you add it at the last minute, and do not let it boil or it will curdle.

WHAT TO KEEP IN YOUR FREEZER

FROZEN BERRIES Berries can make any dessert special, and by using frozen ones it means you don't have to wait until berry season in order to indulge. Try berries such as blueberries, raspberries and strawberries.

FROZEN YOGHURT This is a fantastic substitute for ice-cream and some products even have a similar creamy texture, but with much less fat.

FROZEN VEGETABLES Keep a packet of peas, beans, corn, spinach or mixed vegetables in the freezer—these are handy to add to a quick meal.

ICE-CREAM Reduced or low fat ice-cream is ideal for a quick dessert, served with fresh fruit.

MAKING SENSE OF FOOD LABELLING

These days, food labels contain quite a lot of detailed product information, but unfortunately, very few people know how to interpret it correctly. Often the claims on the front of the packet don't mean quite what you think. Here are some prime examples:

CHOLESTROL FREE Take care, as the food may still be high in fat.

FAT REDUCED Double-check if the product is actually low in fat. Even though the fat may be reduced, it may still be very high.

NO ADDED SUGAR This does not necessarily mean that a product is low in sugar—it could still raise your blood glucose levels.

LITE Check to see exactly what the product is light in. The 'lite' could simply mean light in colour.

The GI logo on food is your guarantee that the product meets the GI Symbol Program's strict nutritional criteria, and has been tested for its GI in an accredited laboratory. This Program was established by the University of Sydney, Diabetes Australia and the Juvenile Diabetes Research Foundation, whose expertise in GI is recognised around the world. The Program is committed to a global vision of healthier populations through nutritionally balanced lower GI diets.

So, for healthier lifestyle choices you can trust, look for the authentic GI symbol when you're shopping. For more information and the latest list of approved products, visit us at: www.gisymbol.com and www.glycemicindex.com.

Ⓖ © ® and ™ University of Sydney in Australia and other countries. All rights reserved.

ACKNOWLEDGEMENTS

A book such as this just doesn't happen. It evolved with the help and inspiration of many individuals. Firstly, we would like to thank the ever cheerful, dedicated and totally tireless production team at Hodder Australia. In particular, our thanks to Fiona Hazard and Anna Waddington for making it all happen; our editor, Kim Rowney, for her commitment and meticulous attention to detail; and Michelle Cutler, for designing a book that is a joy to read.

We are thrilled with the photography and would like to thank Ian Hofstetter, Stephanie Souvlis and Lee Currie. Thank you also to our lovely models: Anna, Bill, Claudia and Jack, Fiona and Sophie, Joanna and Oliver, Julie, Tania, Tyson and Pia, and Vivien. And for supplying the linen and kitchenware for photography, we would like to thank Cloth, Plenty Homewares, and Wheel and Barrow.

As we said at the beginning of the book, we are deeply indebted to all those who have generously provided delicious recipes for this book. In particular we want to thank:

Johanna Burani, our dedicated US colleague, who has adapted a number of our books for the American market, for Chocolate apple sauce cupcakes, page 144; and Cherry oat crunchies, page 156.

Chris and Carolyn Caldicott (www.worldcafe.com) for Sweet potatoes in ginger, cayenne and peanut sauce, page 130, from World Food Café, Bay Books/Soma 1999—a favourite recipe of our North American colleagues, Professor Tom Wolever and his wife, Judy.

Antonio Carluccio for Pasta with cauliflower and pancetta (original title: Cavatelli e cavofiore—Pasta and cauliflower), page 105, from Antonio Carluccio's Vegetables, Headline 2000.

Judy Davie (www.thefoodcoach.com.au) for Beefburgers with (tomato and bean) salsa, page 53; and Scottish oatcakes, page 152, from The Food Coach, Viking 2004.

Jenny Fanshaw for Soba noodle soup with prawns and tofu, page 87; and Apple and strawberry crumble, page 155.

Margaret Fulton for Vegetable chilli bowl, page 51, from Margaret Fulton's New Cookbook, Angus & Robertson 1993.

Liz and Ian Hemphill of Herbies Spices (www.herbies.com.au) for Chachouka, page 48 (with grainy toast), from Spice Notes, Macmillan 2000. Tagine spice mix, page 99; Chermoula spice mix, Harissa, and Vindaloo curry powder, page 162, from Spicery (with Philippa Sandall), Hardie Grant 2004.

Penny Hunking (www.energise.co.uk), who helped adapt The Low GI Diet for the UK, for Barley and vegetable soup, page 75.

Julie Le Clerc (www.julieleclerc.com) for Mustard-roasted fruits, page 36, from Simple Deli Food, Penguin Books (NZ) 2002; and Roast pumpkin and chickpea salad, page 72, from Simple Café Food, Penguin Books (NZ) 1999.

Dr Nancy Longnecker for Lentil bruschetta, page 47, from Passion for Pulses, University of Western Australia Press 2000 (www.uwapress.uwa.edu.au).

Isobel McMillan for Traditional Scottish porridge, page 22; Beef stroganoff, page 101; Crunchy-topped lentil loaf, page 131; and Mung bean dhal, page 164.

Jill McMillan for Nasi goreng, page 60; Fragrant bulgur wheat with zest, page 88; and Aduki bean stew, page 107.

Luke Mangan for Chicken, mint and corn soup, page 83; Curried lentil salad, page 84; and Chilli corn salsa, page 113.

Lynne Mullins, a regular food writer for the Sydney Morning Herald's 'Good Living' section for Vietnamese beef soup, page 93; and Chicken and bok choy stir-fry, page 111, from Noodles to Pasta, HarperCollins Publishers, 1999.

Emma Pemberton for her refreshing Grapefruit granita, page 158.

Professor Steffan Rössner and his daughter Sofia for their dinner party recipes—Golden carrot soup, page 77; Marinated steaks (ostrich or kangaroo) with Mexican bean salad (served with grilled asparagus and bourbon sauce), page 123; and Italian strawberries, page 140.

Emma Sandall for her delicious Couscous salad, page 82.

Catherine Saxelby (www.foodwatch.com.au), our ever-generous colleague who helped us get started on our publishing program, for Fresh plum and ricotta strudel, page 143; and Apricot oat munchies, page 150, from Eating for the Healthy Heart, Hardie Grant Books 2001.

Carol Selva Rajah (www.gourmetasiancuisine.com.au) for her aromatic Pork vindaloo, page 114; Barbecued fish tikka, page 117; and Cucumber raita, page 162.

Dr Rosemary Stanton for Toasted muesli, page 33.

Rick Stein for Steamed monkfish with garlic chives and ginger (original title: Steamed monkfish with wild garlic and ginger), page 126, from Rick Stein's Food Heroes: Another Helping, BBC Books 2004.

Michelle Trute (www.cookingwithconscience.com), passionate GI advocate, for Roasted pumpkin and mushroom lasagne, page 120, from Cooking with Conscience Book 1, self published 2002.

Loukie Werle, food writer and food editor for several Australian magazines, for her Smoked salmon and dill with pasta salad, page 78; and Bavette with fresh mussels (original title: Bavette with fresh mussels for summer), page 102, from Trattoria Pasta, Hodder & Stoughton 1993.

INDEX

Text copyright © 2005 Jennie Brand-Miller, Kaye Foster-Powell and Joanna McMillan-Price
Recipes copyright © 2005 pp. 144, 156 Johanna Burani; p. 130 Chris and Carolyn Caldicott; p. 105 Antonio Carluccio; pp. 53, 152 Judy Davie; p. 51 Margaret Fulton; pp. 48, 99 (Tagine spice mix), 162 Liz and Ian Hemphill; p. 75 Penny Hunking; pp. 36, 72 Julie Le Clerc; p. 47 Dr Nancy Longnecker; pp. 22, 101, 131, 164 Isobel McMillan; pp. 60, 88, 107 Jill McMillan; pp. 83, 84, 113 Luke Mangan; pp. 93, 111 Lynne Mullins; p. 158 Emma Pemberton; pp. 77, 123, 140 Professor Steffan Rössner; pp. 143, 150 Catherine Saxelby; pp. 114, 117, 162 Carol Selva Rajah; p. 33 (Toasted muesli) Dr Rosemary Stanton; p. 126 Rick Stein; p. 120 Michelle Trute; pp. 78, 102 Loukie Werle.

Photography copyright © 2005 Hachette Livre Australia Pty Limited
Photography copyright © 2005 p. 36 Shaun Cato-Symonds; p. 51 John Lee; p. 105 Tim Winter; p. 126 James Murphy; p. 143 Andre Martin.

First published by Hodder Australia
(An imprint of Hachette Livre Australia Pty Limited)

First published in Great Britain in 2005 by Hodder and Stoughton
A division of Hodder Headline
This United Kingdom edition is published by arrangement with Hodder Australia

The right of Jennie Brand-Miller, Kaye Foster-Powell and Joanna McMillan-Price to be identified as the Authors of the Work has been asserted by them in accordance with the Copyright, Designs and Patents Act 1988

A Mobius book

10 9 8 7 6 5

A CIP catalogue record for this title is available from the British Library

ISBN 0 340 89788 0

Designer: Michelle Cutler
Editor: Kim Rowney
Photographer: Ian Hofstetter
Stylist (recipes): Stephanie Souvlis
Home economist: Lee Currie

Typeset in Frutiger and Helvetica

Printed and bound in the UK by CPI Bath
Colour separation by Colourscan, Singapore

Hodder and Stoughton Ltd
A division of Hodder Headline
338 Euston Road
London NW1 3BH

NOTE

The recipes in this book use 20 ml (1/2 fl oz) tablespoon and 250 ml (9 fl oz) cup measures. All cup and spoon measures are level.

Our recipes use large eggs with an average of 60 g (2 oz). All herbs used in the recipes are fresh unless otherwise stated.